The Golem presents a view of science as fallible and untidy, a matter of craft rather than logic. To do this it examines a series of experiments, some famous, such as the proofs of relativity theory, and some not so famous. In each case it shows that scientific certainties do not come from experimental method, but from the way ambiguous results were interpreted.

To explain science the authors display science. Readers should prepare themselves to learn two things: a little *of* science – of the science of relativity, of the centre of the sun, of cosmic forces, of the brains of worms and rats, of the invention of germs, of cold fusion, and of lizards' sex lives – and a lot *about* science – how experiments are really done and how scientific conclusions are reached. The essential fallibility of even so called crucial experiments is displayed.

The Golem: what everyone should know about science

The Golem

what everyone should know about science

HARRY COLLINS

Professor of Sociology and Director of the Science Studies Centre at the University of Bath

TREVOR PINCH

Associate Professor in the Department of Science and Technology Studies at Cornell University

CAMBRIDGE UNIVERSITY PRESS

Published in India by
Foundation Books
2/19 Ansari Road
Darya Ganj
New Delhi-110 002

First Indian Edition 1993

ISBN 81-85618-23-2

This edition of *Harry Collins & Trevor Pinch; The Golem; what everyone should know about science* is published by arrangement with Cambridge University Press, The Edinburgh Building, Shaftesbury Road, Cambridge CB2 2RU, U.K.

Published by Manas Saikia for Foundation Books and printed at Gopsons Papers Pvt. Ltd., A-28, Sector IX, Noida - 201301

To the memory of

SIDNEY COLLINS

and

for **JOAN PINCH**

Contents

Preface and acknowledgements

This book is for the general reader who wants to know how science really works and to know how much authority to grant to experts; it is for the student studying science at school or university; and it is for those at the very beginning of a course in the history, philosophy or sociology of science. In sum, the book is for the citizen living in a technological society. The book adapts the work of professional historians and sociologists for a more general audience. The chapters are of different origins. Some are based on our own work and some on our readings of a selection of the few books and papers in the history and sociology of science that adopt a non-retrospective approach. In these later cases we have relied on the original authors for additional information, and have had occasional resource to archival material. In choosing chapters to represent science we have been limited by the materials to hand. But, given this constraint, we have covered the ground in two ways. We have selected from the life sciences and the physical sciences and we have selected episodes of famous science alongside relatively mundane science and what some would call bad science. We have done this because we want to show that, in terms of our concerns, the science is the same whether it is famous or infamous, big or small, foundational or ephemeral.

Chapter 5 on gravity waves and chapter 7 on solar neutrinos are based on our own original field studies in the sociology of scientific knowledge. The quotations included in these chapters, where not otherwise referenced, are taken from interviews conducted by us with the principal scientists in the areas in question. The interviews concerning the search for gravitational radiation were conducted by Collins between 1972 and 1975. Pinch interviewed solar neutrino scientists in the second half of the 1970s. More complete accounts of this work have been published in other places, notably, Collins' book, *Changing Order: Replication and Induction in Scientific Practice*, and Pinch's book, *Confronting Nature: The Sociology of Solar-Neutrino Detection*.

Chapter 1, on memory transfer, is based on a PhD thesis entitled 'Memories and Molecules' by David Travis, completed with Collins at the University of Bath. Travis was able to read and comment in detail on earlier drafts of the chapter.

The remaining chapters rest on our use of less direct sources of evidence. Chapter 3 on cold fusion is based on Pinch's readings of two books: Frank Close, *Too Hot to Handle: The Race for Cold Fusion* and Eugene Mallove, *Fire From Ice: Searching for the Truth Behind The Cold Fusion Furore*. Pinch also used Thomas Gieryn's paper, 'The Ballad of Pons and Fleischmann: Experiment and Narrative in the (Un)Making of Cold Fusion' and Bruce Lewenstein's paper, 'Cold Fusion and Hot History', and the Cold Fusion Archives held at Cornell University.

For chapter 2 Collins used Loyd Swenson's book, *The Ethereal Aether: A History of the Michelson–Morley–Miller Aether-Drift Experiments, 1880–1930*, and a series of papers. These included Dayton Miller's 1933 publication 'The Ether Drift Experiment and the Determination of the Absolute Motion of the Earth', John Earman and Clark Glymour's 'Relativity and Eclipses: The British Eclipse Expeditions of 1919 and their Predecessors', and H. Von Kluber's 'The Determination of Einstein's Light-deflection in the Gravitational Field of the Sun'. Collins was also helped by personal correspondence with Klaus Hentschel. For chapter 4 Collins used *Louis Pasteur: Free Lance of Science*, by Rene Dubos, and the paper by John Farley and Gerald Geison entitled 'Science Politics and Spontaneous Generation in Nineteenth-Century France: the Pasteur–Pouchet Debate'. (Page references in the text of this chapter refer to the reprint of Farley and Geison's paper in *The Sociology of Scientific Knowledge: A Sourcebook*, edited by Collins.) Collins also referred to the *Dictionary of Scientific Biography*, and consulted some original papers of Pasteur and Pouchet.

For chapter 6, on the sex life of lizards, Pinch relied on Greg Myers's, *Writing Biology: Texts in the Social Construction of Scientific Knowledge*.

The conclusion draws heavily on the last chapter of Collins' book *Changing Order*, on Paul Atkinson and Sarah Delamont's paper 'Mock-ups and Cock-ups: The Stage Management of Guided Discovery Instruction', and on the paper by Collins and Shapin entitled 'Experiment, Science Teaching and the New History and Sociology of Science'.

All the above-mentioned works are fully referenced in the bibliography.

For help and advice we thank David Travis, Lloyd Swenson, Clark Glymour, Klaus Hentschel, Bruce Lewenstein, Gerry Geison, Peter Dear, Pearce Williams, David Crews, Peter Taylor, Shiela Jasanoff, Greg Myers, Paul Atkinson, Frank Close, Eugene Mallove, Sarah Delamont and Steven Shapin. None of them are to blame for the mistakes we may have made in translating their professional work into our words, or in interpreting their findings in our way.

Introduction: the golem

Science seems to be either all good or all bad. For some, science is a crusading knight beset by simple-minded mystics while more sinister figures wait to found a new fascism on the victory of ignorance. For others it is science which is the enemy; our gentle planet, our feel for the just, the poetic and the beautiful, are assailed by a technological bureaucracy – the antithesis of culture – controlled by capitalists with no concern but profit. For some, science gives us agricultural self-sufficiency, cures for the crippled, and a global network of communication; for others it gives us weapons of war, a school teacher's fiery death as the space shuttle falls from grace, and the silent, deceiving, bone-poisoning, Chernobyl.

Both these ideas of science are wrong and dangerous. The personality of science is neither that of a chivalrous knight nor that of a pitiless juggernaut. What, then, is science? Science is a golem.

A golem is a creature of Jewish mythology. It is a humanoid made by man from clay and water, with incantations and spells. It is powerful. It grows a little more powerful every day. It will follow orders, do your work, and protect you from the ever threatening enemy. But it is clumsy and dangerous. Without control, a golem may destroy its masters with its flailing vigour.

The idea of a golem takes on different connotations in different legends. In some the golem is terrifyingly evil, but there is a more homely tradition: in the Yiddish brought from the East European ghetto, a golem (pronounced 'goilem' in that dialect), is a metaphor for any lumbering fool who knows neither his own strength nor the extent of his clumsiness and ignorance. For Collins' grandmother it was good to know a golem if you wanted the garden dug up, but the children were advised to stay clear. Such a golem is not a fiendish devil, it is a bumbling giant.

Since we are using a golem as a metaphor for science, it is also worth noting that in the mediaeval tradition the creature of clay was animated by having the Hebrew 'EMETH', meaning truth, inscribed on its forehead – it is truth that drives it on. But this does not mean it understands the truth – far from it.

The idea of this book is to explain the golem that is science. We aim to show that it is not an evil creature but it is a little daft. Golem Science is not to be blamed for its mistakes; they are our mistakes. A golem cannot be blamed if it is doing its best. But we must not expect too much. A golem, powerful though it is, is the creature of our art and our craft.

The book is very straightforward. To show what Golem Science is, we are going to do something almost unheard of; we are going to display science, with as little reflection on scientific method as we can muster. We are simply going to describe episodes of science, some well known, and some not so well known. We are going to say what happened. Where we do reflect, as in the cold-fusion story, it will be reflection on matters human not methodological. The results will be surprising. The shock comes because the idea of science is so enmeshed in philosophical analyses, in myths, in theories, in hagiography, in smugness, in heroism, in superstition, in fear, and, most important, in perfect hindsight, that what actually happens has never been told outside of a small circle.

Prepare to learn two things. Prepare to learn of little *of* science – of the science of relativity, of the centre of the sun, of cosmic forces, of the brains of worms and rats, of the invention of germs, of cold fusion, and of lizards' sex lives. And prepare to learn a lot *about* science – to learn to love the bumbling giant for what it is.

At the end of the book we'll tell you what we think you should have learned and what the implications are when Golem Science is put to work. The main stuff of the book is in chapters 1–7, which describe episodes (case studies) of science. Each is self-contained and they can be read in any order. The conclusion too can be read at any time, though it will not be convincing outside the setting of the case studies. Whether it is best to read the case studies first, the conclusion first, or something in-between, we do not know; readers can decide for themselves.

We have done very little in the way of explicit analysis of the process of science. Nevertheless, there are common themes that crop up in every chapter, the most important of which is the idea of the 'experimenter's regress'; it is spelt out in chapter 5, on gravitational radiation. The problem with experiments is that they tell you nothing unless they are competently done, but in controversial science no-one can agree on a criterion of competence. Thus, in controversies, it is invariably the case that scientists disagree not only about results, but also about the quality of each other's work. This is what stops experiments being decisive and gives rise to the regress. Readers who would like to go into more detail should refer to the books by Collins and by Pinch mentioned in the 'Preface and Acknowledgements'. The point is that, for citizens who want to take part in the democratic process of a technological society, all the science they need to know about is controversial; thus, it is all subject to the experimenter's regress.

It may be that our conclusions are too unpalatable for some, in which case we hope the descriptions are interesting and informative in their own right. Each case study describes a piece of beautiful scientific work. But the beauty is not the gloss of the philosopher's polishing wheel; it is the glint of rough diamond.

I

Edible knowledge: the chemical transfer of memory

Introduction

Everyone is fascinated by memory and nearly everyone feels that they would prefer their memory to be a little better. Memorising lines in a play, or memorising multiplication tables, is the kind of hard work that people like to avoid. The slow growth of experience that counts as wisdom seems to be the gradual accumulation of memories over a lifetime. If only we could pass on our memories directly we could use our creative abilities from an early age without needing to spend years building the foundations first.

Between the late 1950s and the mid-1970s it began to look as though one day we might be able to build our memories without the usual effort. This was as a result of experiments done by James V. McConnell and, later, Georges Ungar, on the chemical transfer of memory in worms and rats. If memories are encoded in molecules then, in principle, it should be possible to transfer *The Complete Works of Shakespeare* to memory by ingesting a pill, to master the multiplication tables by injection into the bloodstream, or to become fluent in a foreign language by having it deposited under the skin; a whole new meaning would be given to the notion of 'swallowing the dictionary'. McConnell and Ungar believed they had shown that memories were stored in chemicals that could be transferred from animal to animal. They believed they had shown that substances corresponding to memories could be extracted from the brain of one creature and given to a second creature with beneficial effects. If the first creature had been trained in a task, such as turning left or right in an alley in order to reach food, the second creature would know how to reach the food without training – or, at least, with less than the usual amount of training. The second creature would have, as one might say, 'a head start', compared with one which had not had the benefit of the substance corresponding to the memory.

Worms

The first experiments were done by McConnell on planarian worms, a type of flatworm. McConnell trained them to scrunch up their bodies in response to light. He shone a bright light on the worms as they swam along the bottom of a trough, and then gave them a mild shock which caused their bodies to arch or 'scrunch'. Eventually the worms learned to associate light with shock and began to scrunch when a light was shone upon them whether or not the shock was delivered. Worms that scrunched in response to light alone counted as 'trained' worms. This is how McConnell described the experiments

> Imagine a trough gouged out of plastic, 12 inches in length, semicircular in cross-section, and filled with pond water. At either end are brass electrodes attached to a power source. Above the trough are two electric light bulbs. Back and forth in the trough crawls a single flatworm, and in front of the apparatus sits the experimenter, his eye on the worm, his hands on two switches. When the worm is gliding smoothly in a straight line on the bottom of the trough, the experimenter turns on the lights for 3 seconds. After the light has been on for two of the three seconds, the experimenter adds one second of electric shock, which passes through the water and causes the worm to contract. The experimenter records the behaviour of the worm during the two-second period after the light has come on but before the shock has started. If the animal gives a noticeable turning movement or a contraction prior to the onset to the shock this is scored as a 'correct' or 'conditioned' response. *(McConnell, 1962, p.42)*

Now this sounds fairly straightforward but it is necessary to go into detail from the very beginning. Planarian worms scrunch their bodies and turn their heads from time to time even if they are left alone. They will also scrunch in response to many stimuli, including bright light. To train the worms, McConnell had first to discover the level of light that was bright enough for the worms to sense, but not so bright as to cause them to scrunch without the electric shock. Since worm behaviour varies from time to time and from worm to worm we are immediately into statistics rather than unambiguous yes's and no's. What is worse, the effectiveness of the shock training depends upon the worm not being scrunched when the shock is delivered. A worm that is already scrunched has no response left to make to light and shock, and therefore experiences no increment in its training regime when the stimulus is administered. It turns out, then, that to train worms well, it is necessary to watch them carefully and deliver the stimuli only when they are swimming calmly. All these aspects of worm training require skill – skill that McConnell and his assistants built up slowly over a period. When McConnell began his experiments in the 1950s he found that if he trained worms with 150 'pairings' of light followed by shock it resulted in a 45% scrunch response rate to light alone. In the 1960s, by which time he and his associates had become much more practised, the same number of pairings produced a 90% response rate.

In the mid-1950s McConnell tried cutting trained worms in half. The planarian worm can regenerate into a whole worm from either half of a dissected specimen. McConnell was interested in whether worms that regenerated from the front half, containing the putative brain, would retain the training. They did, but the real surprise was that worms regenerated from the brain-less rear half did at least as well if not better. This suggested that the training was somehow distributed throughout the worm, rather than being localised in the brain. The idea emerged that the training might be stored chemically.

McConnell tried to transfer training by grafting parts of trained worms to untrained specimens, but these experiments met with little success. Some planarian worms are cannibalistic. McConnell next tried feeding minced portions of trained worms to their naive brothers and sisters and found that those who had ingested trained meat were about one-and-a-half times more likely to respond to light alone than they otherwise would be. These experiments were being reported around 1962. By now, the notion that memory could be *transferred* by chemical means was the driving force of the experiments.

Arguments about the worm experiments

Transplantation versus chemical transfer

The notion that training or memory could be transferred by chemical means gave rise to substantial controversy. One counter argument was to agree that training was being transferred between worm and worm but to argue that it had no great significance. The planarian worm has a digestive system that is quite different from that of a mammal. The worm's digestive system does not break down its food into small chemical components but rather incorporates large components of ingested material into its body. To speak loosely, it might be that the naive worms were being given 'implants' of trained worm – either bits of brain, or some other kind of distributed memory structure – rather than absorbing memory substance. This would be interesting but would not imply that memory was a chemical phenomenon and, in any case, would probably have no significance for our understanding of memory in mammals. McConnell's response to this was to concentrate on what he believed was the memory substance. Eventually he was injecting naive worms with RNA extracted from trained creatures, and claiming considerable success.

Sensitisation versus training

Another line of attack rested on the much more basic argument that planarian worms were too primitive to be trained. According to this line, McConnell had fooled himself into thinking that he had trained the worms to respond to light, whereas he had merely increased their general level of sensitivity to all stimuli. If anything was being transferred between worm and worm, it was a sensitising substance rather than something that carried a specific memory.

It is difficult to counter this argument because any kind of training regime is likely to increase sensitivity. Training is done by 'pairing' exposure to light with electric shock. One way of countering the sensitisation hypothesis is to subject the worms to the same number of shocks and bursts of light, but in randomised order. If sensitisation is the main effect, then worms subjected to a randomised pattern of shocks and light bursts should be just as likely to scrunch in response to light alone as worms subjected to properly organised pairings of stimuli. If it is training rather than sensitisation that is important, the trained worms will do better.

Once more, this sounds simple. Indeed, McConnell and other 'worm runners' did find a significant difference between *trained* and *sensitised* worms, but the effect is difficult to repeat because training is a matter of *skilled practice*. As explained above, to effect good training it is necessary to observe the worms closely and learn to understand when they are calm enough for a shock to produce a training increment. Different trainers may obtain widely differing outcomes from training regimes however much they try to repeat the experiments according to the specification.

To the critic, the claim that a poor result is the outcome of poor training technique – specifically, a failure to understand the worms – sounds like an *ad hoc* excuse. To say that only certain technicians understand the worms well enough to be able to get a result sounds like a most unscientific argument. Critics always think that the claim that only some people are able to get results – the 'golden hands' argument, as one might call it – is *prima facie* evidence that something unsound is going on. And there are many cases in the history of science where a supposedly golden-handed experimenter has turned out to be a fraud. Nevertheless, the existence of specially skilful experimenters – the one person in a lab who can successfully manage an extraction or a delicate measurement – is also widely attested. In the field of pharmacology, for example, the 'bioassay' is widely used. In a bioassay, the existence and quantity of a drug is determined by its effects on living matter or whole organisms. In a sense, the measurement of the effect of various brain extracts on worms and rats could be seen as itself a bioassay rather than a transfer experiment. Yet the bioassay is a technique that has the reputation of being potentially difficult to 'transfer' from one group of scientists to another because it requires so much skill and practice. It is, then, very hard to separate golden hands from *ad hocery*, a problem that has a particular salience in this field. Certainly attributions of dishonesty are not always appropriate.

For this kind of reason the argument between McConnell and his critics was able to drag on, reaching its zenith in 1964 with the publication of a special supplement to the journal, *Animal Behaviour*, devoted to the controversy. At this point it would be hard to say who was winning, but it was clear that McConnell's claim that training worms required special skills was becoming a little more acceptable.

Confounding variables and replication

Sensitisation could be looked at as a confounding variable, and critics put forward a number of others. For example, planarian worms produce slime as they slither along. Nervous worms prefer swimming into slimed areas which have been frequented by other worms. A naive worm swimming in a two-branched alley will naturally prefer to follow the path marked out most strongly by the slime of worms that have gone before. If the alley has been used for training, the preferred route will be that which the trainee worms have used most often. Thus, naive worms might prefer to follow their trained counterparts not because of the transfer of any substance, but because of the slime trails left before. Even in an individual worm it might be that the development of a preference for, say, right turns, might be the build-up of a self-reinforcing slime trail rather than a trained response.

Once this has been pointed out there are a number of remedies. For example, the troughs might be scrubbed between sessions (though it is never quite clear when enough scrubbing has been done), or new troughs might be regularly employed. One critic found that in properly cleaned troughs no learning effect could be discovered, but McConnell, as a result of further research, claimed that worms could not be trained properly in a clean environment. He suggested that worms were unhappy in an environment made unfamiliar because it was free of slime; too much hygiene prevented the experiments working. One can readily imagine the nature of the argument between McConnell and his critics over the effects of sliming.

Eventually, this part of the argument was resolved, at least to McConnell's satisfaction, by pre-sliming training grounds with naive worms that were not part of the experiment. This made the troughs and alleys comfortable for the experimental subjects without reinforcing any particular behaviour.

All these arguments take time, and it is not always clear to everyone exactly what has been established at any point. This is one of the reasons why controversies drag on for so long when the logic of the experiments seems clear and simple. Remember, too, that every experiment requires a large number of trials and a statistical analysis. The levels of the final effects are usually low so it is not always clear just what has been proved.

Whether or not McConnell's results could be replicated by others, or could be said to be replicable, depended on common agreement about what were the important variables in the experiment. We have already discussed the necessity – from McConnell's point of view – of understanding and of skilled handling of the worms. In his own laboratory, the training of 'worm runners' by an experienced scientist was followed by weeks of practice. It was necessary to learn not to 'push the worms too hard'. In his own words:

> [it is necessary to] treat them tenderly, almost with love . . . it seems certain that the variability in success rate from one laboratory to another is due, at least in part, to differences in personality and past experience among the various investigators. *(McConnell, 1965, p.26).*

As explained, to look at it from the critics point of view, this was one of the *excuses* McConnell used in the face of the palpable non-repeatability of his work. The effect of sliming was another variable cited by both proponents and critics in their different ways.

As a scientific controversy develops more variables that might affect the experiments come to the fore. For the proponents these are more reasons why the unpractised might have difficulty in making the experiments work; for the critics, they are more excuses that can be used when others fail to replicate the original findings.

In the case of the worm experiments up to 70 variables were cited at one time or another to account for discrepancies in experimental results. They included: the species and size of the worms; the way they were housed when not undergoing training – was it in the dark or the light?; the type of feeding; the frequency of training; the temperature and chemical composition of the water; the strength of the light, its colour and duration; the nature of the electric shock – its pulse shape, strength, polarity and so forth; the worm's feeding schedule; the season of the year; and the time of day when the worms were trained. Even the barometric pressure, the phase of the moon, and the orientation of the training trough with respect to the earth's magnetic field were cited at one time or another. This provided ample scope for accusation and counter-accusation – skill versus *ad hocery*. The greater the number of potential variables, the harder it is to decide whether one experiment really replicates the conditions of another.

The Worm Runner's Digest

McConnell was an unusual scientist. What people are prepared to believe is not just a function of what a scientist discovers but of the image of the work that he or she presents. McConnell was no respecter of scientific convention and in this he did himself no favours. Among his unconventional acts was founding, in 1959, a journal called *The Worm Runner's Digest*. He claimed this was a way of coping with the huge amount of mail that he received as a result of the initial work on worms, but the *Digest* also published cartoons and scientific spoofs.

Ironically, one of the disadvantages of the worm experiments was that they seemed so easy. It meant that many experimenters, including high school students, could try the transfer tests for themselves. It was these high school students who swamped McConnell with requests for information and accounts of their results. The newsletter, which became *The Worm Runner's Digest*, was McConnell's response.

It is not necessarily a good thing to have high school students repeat one's experiments for it makes them appear to lack *gravitas*. What is worse, it makes it even more difficult than usual to separate serious and competent scientific work from the slapdash or incompetent. It is certainly not a good thing to found a 'jokey' newsletter if you want your work to be taken seriously.

In 1967 the journal split into two halves, printed back to back, with the second half being re-titled *The Journal of Biological Psychology*. This journal was treated in a more conventional way, with articles being refereed. The idea was that the more serious work would appear in the refereed end of the journal while the jokey newsletter material would be reserved for the *Digest* half. (The analogy between the journal and the front and back halves of regenerating worms was not lost on McConnell and the contributors. Which end contained the brain?) *The Journal of Biological Psychology*, refereed though it was, never attained the full respectability of a conventional scientific outlet. How could it with *The Worm Runner's Digest* simultaneously showing its backside to scientific convention in every issue?

Because a number of McConnell's results were published in *The Worm Runner's Digest/The Journal of Biological Psychology* scientists did not know how to take them. To put it another way, any critic who was determined not to take McConnell's work seriously had a good excuse to ignore his claims if their only scientific outlet was in McConnell's own, less than fully attested, journal. In the competition between scientific claims, the manner of presentation is just as important as the content. The scientific community has its ceremonies and its peculiar heraldic traditions. The symbols may be different – Albert Einstein's unruly hair and Richard Feynman's Brooklyn accent in place of gilded lions and rampant unicorns – but the division between scientific propriety and eccentricity is firm if visible only to the enlightened. Much of what McConnell did fell on the wrong side of the line.

The ending of the worm controversy

Around the mid-1960s, as McConnell was beginning to establish that worms could be trained, if not that the transfer phenomenon could be demonstrated, the stakes were changed in such a way as to make some of the earlier arguments seem petty. This was the result of experiments suggesting that the transfer phenomenon could be found in mammals.

Some of McConnell's most trenchant critics had argued that planarian learning was impossible, others that it had not been fully proved. We may be sure that the strong attacks on learning were motivated by the importance of the transfer phenomenon. With the apparent demonstration of transfer in rats and mice, the objections to planarian learning dropped away. Rats and mice are familiar laboratory animals. There is no dispute that they can learn, and there is no dispute that in order to learn they have to be carefully handled. It is acknowledged that the technicians who handle the rats in a psychology or biology laboratory must be skilled at their job. Once the worm experiments were seen through the refracted light of the later experiments on rats it appeared entirely reasonable that worms should need special handling, and entirely reasonable that they could learn. The believers in McConnell's results stressed this, as in the following quotation from two experimenters:

> It seems paradoxical that when we run rats, we handle our subjects, we specify what breeding line the stock is from, we train them in sound-proof boxes, and we specify a large number of factors which when put together give us an output we call learning . . . Planarians on the other hand are popped into a trough, given a . . . [conditioned stimulus] and . . . [an unconditioned stimulus] and are expected to perform like a learning rat. *(Corning and Riccio, 1970, p.129).*

But this kind of *cri de coeur* only came to seem reasonable to the majority at a later date. It only became acceptable when nobody cared very much because their attention had been turned to the much more exciting subject of transfer of behaviour among mammals. This was a much more important challenge to received wisdom about the nature of memory.

Mammals

Early experiments

The first claims to have demonstrated memory transfer in mammals came from four independent groups working without knowledge of each other's research. The first four studies were associated with the names, in alphabetical order, of Fjerdingstad, Jacobson, Reinis, and Ungar. All these studies were being done around 1964, and were published in 1965.

Fjerdingstad placed rats in a training box with two alleyways, one was lit and one was darkened according to a random sequence. The rats were deprived of water for 24 hours, but received a few drops if they entered the illuminated alley. Injections of trained brain extract caused naive rats to prefer the box in which their trained colleagues had found relief from thirst.

Jacobson had hungry rats learn to associate the sound of a clicker with a food reward. The association of clicks with food could, so he claimed, be transferred to naive rats by injection.

Reinis taught rats to take food from a dispenser during the period of a conditioned stimulus – either a light or a buzzer. This expectation, it appeared, could also be transferred by injections.

McConnell's laboratory also began to work on rats in the mid-1960s but, in the long term, the most important mammal experimenter was Georges Ungar. Ungar began by showing that tolerance to morphine could be transferred. As an animal becomes accustomed to a drug it requires greater doses to produce the same effects on its behaviour. This is known as 'tolerance' to the drug. Ungar ground up the brains of 50 tolerant rats and injected an extract into unexposed rats. The result, reported in 1965, seemed to be that the tolerance was transferred. Whether this is to be counted as the transfer of *learning* is not clear. As explained earlier, Ungar might be thought of as doing a complicated bioassay rather than an experiment in the transfer of learning. The significance of this point will become more evident in due course.

Ungar moved on to attempt to transfer 'habituation'. He exposed rats to the sound of a loud bell until they became accustomed to it and ceased to exhibit the usual 'startle reaction'. Habituation too could be transferred, apparently, through injection of brain extract. Interestingly, Ungar transferred the habituation not to rats but from rats to mice.

Early reactions

It is important to get some of the flavour of the early reaction of scientists to these strange and unorthodox results. The following reports of reactions are from 1966, just after the early mammal results had appeared. It is probable that part of the strength of the response was caused by association with the earlier worm experiments.

One scientist reported that after he had given his presentation he found that people 'drifted away from him' in the bar. Other scientists told of similar reactions to the exposure of the transfer results at conferences:

> the nightly private gatherings brought to the surface all the deeply felt emotional objections which, for reasons I have difficulty to understand and analyse, some people have against the whole idea. This was particularly manifest after a few drinks.

> I was stunned. People were really – vicious is maybe too strong a word – but certainly mean . . . It took me quite a while to realize I had trodden on sacred territory. It was 'Why didn't you do this?', 'Why didn't you do that?' . . . it was all accusations.

> . . . it was one of those times when you see the people who are at the absolute cutting edge of a science, all packed together . . . in a smoke-filled room, trying to decide what was right . . . I remember that meeting particularly, because at the end of the evening those people who had gotten positive results were telling the people who had gotten negative results that they were totally incompetent and didn't know how to run an experiment; and the people who had gotten negative results were telling those people who had gotten positive results that they were frauds. That they were faking the data.

Georges Ungar's main work

Ungar's best-known work began in 1967. In these experiments rats had to choose between entering a lighted or a darkened box. A rat's natural preference would be for the dark but on entering the darkened box they were locked in and given a five second electric shock delivered through the metal grid of the floor. The rats learned to avoid the dark box very quickly, but Ungar gave his rats five trials a day, for six to eight days, to make sure that a good supply of the 'fear of the dark' chemical was produced in the rats' brains.

After training, the rats were killed and an extract was prepared from their brains. This was injected into mice, who were tested in the same apparatus. By measuring the proportion of time spent in the light or dark box during a three minute trial it was possible to tell if mice which had been injected with brain extract from trained rats were more likely to avoid the dark than those which had been injected with a similar extract prepared from the brains of normal rats.

Replication in mammals

As explained, all the work on mammals was violently contested and attempts were made both to support and disprove the findings. According to Ungar's rough (and contentious) analysis of published experimental reports between 1965 and 1975, there were 105 positive and 23 negative replications, following the pattern below:

Ungar's analysis of transfer experiments in mammals, 1965–75

	1965	1966	1967	1968	1969	1970	1971	1972	1973	1974	1975
Positive	13	13	13	16	23	17	27	13	23	17	8
Negative	1	6	4	5	1	3	1	1	–	–	1

This is a good point at which to note a feature of science that is often misunderstood. The sheer number and weight of experimental replications is not usually enough to persuade the scientific community to believe in some unorthodox finding. In this case, for example, a single one of the negative experiments, carried out by a number of influential scientists, outweighed the far larger number of positive results. Scientists have to have grounds for believing the result of an experiment – and this is quite reasonable given, as we demonstrate throughout the book, the skill involved. Scientists will demand better grounds where an experiment produces more unorthodox results; one might say that they start with grounds for not believing. Again, among the sorts of grounds people look for in deciding whether or not to believe a result are the scientist's reputation and the respectability of his or her institution. This, of course, militates still more strongly against the unorthodox. Ungar's figures show clearly that experimental replication is not a straightforward business and neither are the conclusions that scientists draw from replications.

Naturally, competing results were supported by competing arguments about the competence and skill of the experimenters. Let us give an example of the 'flavour' of these problems with illustrations from the debate between Ungar and the group at Stanford University.

The debate with Stanford

Stanford attempted to replicate Ungar's work as closely as possible. It was felt that in Ungar's experiments:

> some ... peptide material has evidently been isolated ... if this material – whatever its exact structure or state of purity – is truly capable of specifically transferring a learned behaviour to untrained recipient animals, the discovery ranks among the most fundamental in modern biology. *(Goldstein, 1973, p.60).*

In the event they obtained negative results. Inevitably, this led Ungar to point to residual differences between the Stanford experiments and his own which could account for the failure. In what follows, then, we first see the two series of experiments looking more and more like each other as the Stanford group tried to replicate every detail of Ungar's work, and then the experiments are 'prised apart' again when the unexpected Stanford outcome is reported.

The leader of the Stanford group, Avram Goldstein, first spent three days at Ungar's laboratory to make sure that he could follow the published procedures accurately. In a 1971 publication, the subsequent work of him and his collaborators was described as follows:

> In the next three months we carried out eighteen unsuccessful experiments with 125 donor rats and 383 recipient saline and control mice. We then did a blind test on our mice using control and trained donor extracts provided by Dr. Ungar. Next, we sent 100 of our mice to Houston, for testing as recipients concurrently with the local strain. Finally, we selected, from all our experiments, those mice (of both sexes) which seemed to avoid the black box more often after receiving extracts. These animals were bred and the offspring tested as recipients. We hoped to select for recipient capability that might be under genetic influence. The results of all these experiments were negative.
> *(Goldstein, Sheehan and Goldstein, 1971, p. 126).*

These various collaborations with Ungar's laboratories were meant to eliminate any residual differences between the Stanford procedures and those used by Ungar. Stanford, as was clear from the same publication, were trying their best in an open-minded spirit:

> We should not dismiss the possibility that acquired behaviour . . . can be transferred by brain extracts, merely because the proposed mechanisms . . . seem fanciful, especially since confirmatory results have been published by several laboratories.
> *(Goldstein et al., 1971, p. 129)*

After their failure the tone of the debate changed. The Stanford group suggested that their 'rather exhaustive' attempts showed that the conditions for a successful transfer would have to be specified more exactly.

> Can the investigators state precisely the conditions for carrying out an assay, in such detail that competent scientists elsewhere can reproduce their results? Our own repeated failure . . . could be dismissed as the bungling work of incompetents were it not matched by published experiences of others. *(Goldstein, 1973, p. 61).*

The difference between the two experiments began to emerge. With reference to the interpretation of one aspect of the results, Goldstein and his team noted:

> Because we were unable to agree with Dr. Ungar on the interpretation of the results they are not included here but will presumably be published independently by him. *(Goldstein et al., 1971, p. 129).*

To this, Ungar replied:

> ... some of the most important parameters were arbitrarily changed ... This was certainly not done because he was unaware of our procedures. *(Ungar, 1973, p. 312)*.

Ungar also stated that the Stanford group had 'eliminated one of the three boxes of our testing device, trained some of the donors only once instead of five times ... and used a different strain of mice' (Ungar, 1973, p. 309).

Ungar also objected to the measure of dark avoidance that the Stanford group had used. Rather than presenting the results in terms of the length of time the rats spent in the darkened box, they had measured 'latency'. This is the length of time the mouse is in the apparatus before it *first* enters the dark box. Goldstein stated that he had noted that Ungar also recorded latencies, but always published data in terms of dark box time.

> I thought this curious, because if dark avoidance behaviour were really induced by the injections, the latency would be increased. This is elementary logic. Indeed, latency is the common and accepted measure for such behavioural phenomena among experimental psychologists. Yet Ungar has never used latency ... *(Goldstein, 1973, p. 61)*.

Ungar replied:

> ... in his latest comments, he tries to justify one of these changes, the use of latency, as a criterion of dark avoidance, instead of the total time spent in the dark box. We have shown empirically, and showed it to him, that a number of mice run rapidly into the dark but come out immediately and spend the rest of the time in the light ... latency would, therefore, give misleading results. *(Ungar, 1973, p. 312)*.

Goldstein felt:

> Dark box time ... would probably be sensitive to other behavioural effects. A recipient mouse that wanders around more because it is hyperactive would naturally be more likely to leave the dark box than a passive animal. *(Goldstein, 1973, p. 61)*.

As can be seen, Ungar and Goldstein disagreed about whether enough detail had been published, whether certain differences between the original and the replication were significant, and the appropriateness of different measures of fear of the dark. Ungar saw

Goldstein's work as having departed clearly and significantly from his procedures.

Competing strategies

In so far as the memory transfer technique was important to psychologists, it was important primarily because it seemed to offer a tool for 'dissecting' memory. For many of the psychologists the main hope was that the technique would allow them to take apart some aspects of learning. The precise chemical nature of memory transfer substances was of secondary importance to this group. Thus, McConnell remarked, jokingly, that as far as he was concerned the active material might as well be boot polish.

McConnell and other behavioural psychologists worked to find out whether further memory-related behavioural tendencies could be chemically transferred from mammal to mammal. Fear of the dark might be seen as a general disposition rather than something specific that had been learned.

The *specificity* argument paralleled the sensitisation debate in the case of the worms but was even more salient in the case of mammals. The exciting thing would be if there were specific molecules related to specific memories or learned behaviours. For many, this claim was difficult to accept. Much more palatable was the notion that molecules would have a non-specific effect on behaviour that would vary in different circumstances. For example, suppose the effect of the memory molecule was to alter the overall emotional state of the animal rather than providing it with a particular memory. In such a case, placing an injected but untrained animal in the same circumstances that its dead colleague had experienced in training – say a choice between light and dark – should cause it to produce the response that had been induced during the training – choosing the light. In different circumstances, however, the effect might be quite different; for example, if the injected animal was given a choice between pink and blue boxes it might cause it to bite its tail. If this was what transfer was all about, there would never be a *Complete Works of Shakespeare* pill.

McConnell wanted to find out if what psychologists would count as 'grade-A learning' could be transferred. One might say that proving that something like the works of Shakespeare could exist in chemical form was what drove McConnell on.

To show 'grade-A learning' McConnell and other experimenters taught rats more complex tasks such as the choice of a left or a right turn in an alley in order to get food. These experiments were done in the late 1960s. 'Discrimination' tasks such as these seemed to be transferable among rats as well as other creatures such as cats, goldfish, cockroaches and the praying mantis. A degree of cross-species transfer was also found.

Unlike McConnell, Ungar was a pharmacologist by training and was much more interested in a 'biochemical strategy'. That is, he wanted to isolate, analyse and synthesise active molecules. For Ungar the important thing was to find some reproducible transfer effect and study the chemical that was responsible for it, whether or not the transferred behaviour was grade-A learning. Concentrating on fear of the dark, Ungar set about extracting what became known as 'Scotophobin'. To obtain a measurable amount, he required the brains of 4000 trained rats. This was certainly big, expensive, science as far as psychologists were concerned, and even other biochemists could not compete with him. Eventually Ungar believed he had isolated, analysed and then synthesised Scotophobin.

Ungar had hoped that the problems of repeating chemical transfer experiments would be solved by the availability of the synthetic material but, as so often in contested science, there is so much detail that is contestable that experiments can force no-one to agree that anything significant has been found.

There were disputes over the purity of the synthetic material; its stability and the way it was kept by other laboratories before it was used; and the kind of behavioural changes (if any) it induced. In addition, Ungar announced several alterations to the precise chemical structure of Scotophobin. The upshot was continued controversy. A few of those who believed in the chemical transfer effect felt that there was a 'family' of Scotophobin-like chemicals for different species, with similar but slightly different formulae. One experiment showed that the synthetic version of Scotophobin had no effect on mice, but produced dark avoidance in goldfish!

It is difficult to be precise about the numbers of experiments on synthetic Scotophobin that were completed, since different synthetic versions were produced, many results were never published, and some of these were concerned only with testing exactly where the material ended up in the recipient's brain. Several dozens of experiments are known, but there is sufficient ambiguity for both believers and sceptics to draw comfort from the results.

The end of the story

McConnell closed his laboratory in 1971. He was unable to obtain further funding for the work and, in any case, he could see that to prove the transfer effect it would be necessary to adopt an Ungar-like strategy of isolating and synthesising the active agents. Ungar, one might say, had won the competition over experimental strategy. The psychologists had lost out to the 'big science' of biochemistry.

Ungar pressed ahead with his programme of research. Training thousands of rats was too large a project to be done frequently, and he turned his attention to goldfish. Goldfish are good at colour discrimination tasks and are relatively cheap. Nearly 17 000 trained goldfish gave their lives in the production of about 750 grams of colour discriminating brains but this was still insufficient for him to identify the chemical structure of the putative memory substances, 'chromodiopsins'.

Ungar, who was of normal retiring age when he began the work on transfer, died in 1977 at the age of 71 and the field died with him. It was Ungar's very dominance of the field, brought about by his ambitious approach, that had killed off competing laboratories. On the one hand there was never quite enough reliability in the transfer effect to make the experiments really attractive to a beginner or someone short of resources; on the other hand, Ungar had raised the stakes so much that the investment required to make a serious attempt at repeating his work was too high. Thus when Ungar died there was no-one to take over the mantle.

Ungar left behind a number of formulae for behaviourally active molecules that were the result of his work on rats and goldfish. Some scientists tried to synthesise Scotophobin and test it on animals but, as noted above, tests on Scotophobin did not provide any clear answer to the question of whether it really was the chemical embodiment of 'fear of the dark' or something more general such as fear. In any case, if Ungar's heroic efforts did have valuable implications, they were lost to view when the related field of brain-peptide chemistry exploded in the late 1970s. Scientists now had brain chemicals to work on which had clear effects, but effects unrelated to memory transfer.

Scotophobin thus lost its special salience and its historical relationship to the disreputable transfer phenomenon became a disadvantage. Most scientists, then, simply forgot about the area. Like many controversies, it ended with a whimper rather than a bang.

It is hard to say that any particular experiment or set of experiments demonstrated the non-existence of the transfer phenomenon, but three publications seemed decisive at the time. Their *historical* interest lies in the negative effect they had when they were published while one might say that their *sociological* interest lies in the reasons for that effect, especially given that in retrospect they appear much less decisive.

The first paper was published in 1964 and came from the laboratory of Nobel Laureate Melvin Calvin (Bennett and Calvin, 1964); it concerned planarian worms. The paper described a series of experiments – some employing McConnell's ex-students to perform the training – that seemed to show that learning had not taken place. This paper had a powerful effect, and for many years was quoted as undermining the early research on the chemical transfer of memory. Today, its cautious verdict that learning was 'not yet proven' has been superseded and it is accepted that worms not only turn, but learn.

The second paper, by Byrne and 22 others, was published in 1966 (Byrne *et al.*, 1966). It was a short piece in *Science* reporting the failure of the attempts by seven different laboratories to replicate one of the early chemical transfer experiments. Again, it is often cited as a 'knockdown blow' to the field. Indeed, it was at the time. But for Ungar, and other proponents, all of the experiments mentioned in the paper – and the original experiment they attempted to replicate – are flawed because they assumed the transfer material to be RNA rather than a peptide. According to Ungar, the chemical techniques used by the replicators in treating the brain extract probably destroyed the active, peptide, material. On this account, the original experiment, fortuitously, used *poor* biochemical techniques and, failing to destroy the peptide, obtained the correct positive result!

The last paper is the best known. Ungar's five-page report of his analysis and synthesis of Scotophobin was published in *Nature*, perhaps the highest prestige journal for the biological sciences (Ungar *et al.*, 1972). Accompanying it, however, was a critical, fifteen-page, signed report by the referee. The detailed critical comments of the referee, and perhaps the mere fact of this exceptional form of publication significantly reduced the credibility of the memory transfer phenomenon. It is worth noting that *Nature* has used this unusual form of publication subsequently to the disadvantage of other pieces of fringe science and, perhaps, to the disadvantage of science as a whole.

In spite of the widespread demise of the credibility of the chemical transfer of memory, a determined upholder of the idea would find no published disproof that rests on decisive technical evidence. For such a person it would not be unreasonable or unscientific to start experimenting once more. Each negative result can be explained away while many of the positive ones have not been. In this, memory transfer is an exemplary case of controversial science. We no longer believe in memory transfer but this is because we tired of it, because more interesting problems came along, and because the principal experimenters lost their credibility. Memory transfer was never quite disproved; it just ceased to occupy the scientific imagination. The gaze of the golem turned elsewhere.

2

Two experiments that 'proved' the theory of relativity

INTRODUCTION TO PARTS 1 AND 2

Einstein's theory of relativity became widely known in the early part of the twentieth century. One of the reasons for its success among scientists was that it made sense of a number of puzzling observations. For example, the theory accounted for the orbit of the planet Mercury departing slightly from its expected path, and it made sense of a slight shift towards the red end of the spectrum which some had claimed to detect in the light coming from the sun. But the theory of relativity also achieved a popular success; it became the subject of newspaper headlines. This had something to do with the ending of the Great War and the unifying effect of science on a fractured continent. It had something to do with the dramatic circumstances and the straightforward nature of the 1919 'proof' of relativity. And it undoubtedly had something to do with the astonishing consequences of the theory for our common-sense understanding of the physical world. When the implications of Einstein's insight – that light must travel at the same speed in all directions – were worked out, strange things were predicted.

It turned out that, if Einstein's ideas are correct, time, mass, and length are not fixed but are relative to the speed at which things move. Things that go very fast – at speeds near to the velocity of light – would get very heavy and very short. People who travelled this fast would seem to everyone else to age slowly; identical twins could grow old at different rates if one stayed still and one went on a very rapid journey. If the theory is correct, light would not travel only in straight lines, but would be bent by gravitational fields to a greater extent than had been believed possible. A more sinister consequence of the theory was that mass and energy should be interchangeable. On the one hand this explained how the sun kept on burning even though its fuel should have been exhausted long ago. On the other hand, terrible new sources of power became possible, a consequence to be demonstrated later by evidence for which the adjective 'incontrovertible' might have been invented – the explosion of the atomic bomb. In so far as there are facts of science, the relationships between matter and energy put forward by Einstein are facts.

But the explosion of the atomic bomb in 1945 is not what 'proved' the theory of relativity. It had been accepted for many years before then. The way the story is most often told is that there were two decisive observational proofs. These were the Michelson–Morley 'aether-drift' experiment of the 1880s, which we discuss in part 1 of this chapter, and Eddington's 1919 solar eclipse observation of the apparent displacement of stars, which we discuss in part 2.

The conventional story is that the Michelson–Morley observations showed that light travelled at the same speed in all directions, proving the special theory of relativity, while Eddington's expeditions to distant lands to observe the eclipse of 1919 showed that starlight was bent by the sun to the right extent to prove the general theory. The drama lies in the clarity and decisiveness of the questions and the answers. Either light did travel at the same speed in all directions or it did not. Either stars near the sun were displaced twice as far as they should have been under the old Newtonian theory or they were not. On the face of it, nothing could be more straightforward. For many people of that generation, interest in science was fired by the extraordinary nature of relativity and the story of the early observations. But even these experiments turn out to be far less decisive than is generally belived. What is simple 'on the face of it', is far more complicated in practice.

PART 1. DOES THE EARTH SAIL IN AN AETHERIAL SEA?

> In 1887 Albert Michelson and Edward Morley carried out a very careful experiment at the Case School for Applied Science in Cleveland. They compared the speed of light in the direction of the earth's motion with that at right angles to the earth's motion. To their surprise, they found they were exactly the same!
> *(Stephen Hawking,* A Brief History of Time: From the Big Bang to Black Holes, *Bantam Books, 1988, p. 20).*

The tranquil aether sea

Light and the aether

In the latter part of the nineteenth century it was believed that light waves travel through a universal if insubstantial medium called the 'aether'. If this were true, then the velocity of light waves would appear to vary as the earth moves through the aether in its orbit round the sun. Just as when you run fast in still air you create your own breeze, the movement of the earth should create its own 'aether wind' in the tenuous 'aether sea'. Stand on the surface of the earth looking into the wind, and light coming toward you should appear to move faster than it would if the aether were still. The speed of light should be increased by the speed of the aether wind. Look across the wind, however, and light should appear to move at its normal speed. When Albert A. Michelson conducted his early experiments on the aether wind this is what he expected to find; what he actually found was that light seemed to move at the same velocity in all directions.

Michelson and relativity

According to the theory of relativity, light *should* have a constant velocity in all directions, but the theory did not surface until some 25 years after Michelson began his observations. Michelson, then, knew nothing of relativity; he set out to use movement through the aether sea as a kind of speedometer for the earth. Although the experiment is often thought of as giving rise to a problem that Einstein set out to solve, this too is probably false. It appears that Einstein was little interested in Michelson's experiments when he formulated his theory. Einstein's starting point was a paradox in the theory of electrical waves. The link between Einstein and Michelson was forged by others some twenty or more years after the first 'decisive' experiments were completed. Michelson, then, had no idea of the importance his results were later to achieve. At the time he was disappointed, for he had failed to find the speed of the earth. As we shall see, Michelson did not even complete the experiments properly; he went straight on to other things after publishing the initial findings.

How to measure the speed of the aether wind

To measure the velocity of the earth Michelson needed to measure the velocity of light in a variety of directions. The starting assumption was that the maximum speed of the earth with respect to the aether was of the order of the speed of the planet's movement in its orbit around the sun: about 18.5 miles per second. The speed of light was known to be in the region of 185 000 miles per second, so the effect to be measured was small – one part in 10 000. What is worse, direct determinations of the speed of light were too inaccurate to allow such a small discrepancy to be seen, so the only possibility was to compare the speed in two directions.

The method was to use what we now call 'interferometry'. The same beam of light is split into two and recombined. When the split beam recombines it will give rise to 'interference fringes': a series of light and dark bands. The effect is due to the light *waves* in each half of the beam alternately reinforcing each other (the bright bands) and cancelling each other out (the dark bands). This is a simple geometrical consequence of the superimposition of two wave motions: as one moves across the field upon which the rays converge, the path length of each ray changes slightly. For example, the left hand ray (Ray 1 in figure 2.1) has to travel a certain distance to reach the left hand side of the illuminated area. To reach a point a little to the right, it will have to travel slightly further, and to reach a point on the far right hand

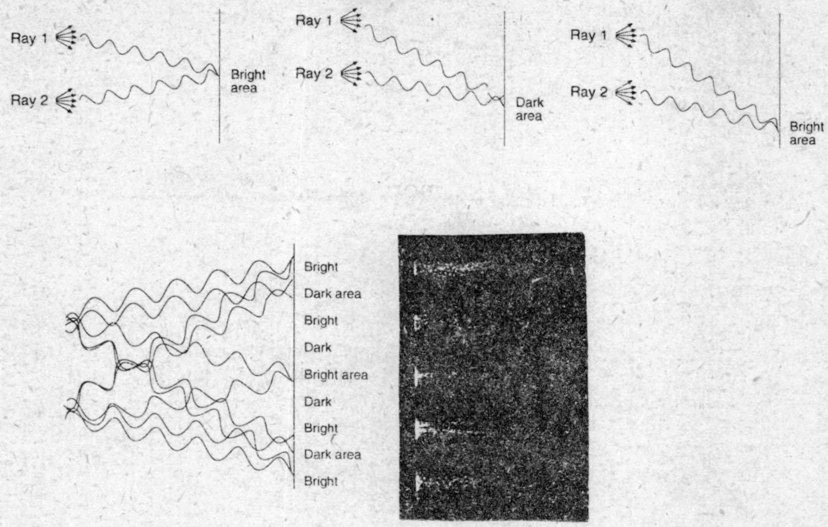

Figure 2.1. Interference fringes.

side of the field it will have to travel still further. Thus the ray will strike the field at various different stages in its undulation; the peak of Ray 1 strikes one point of the field whereas the trough strikes another point a little further along. Since the same applies to Ray 2, both peaks (or troughs) will strike the same point sometimes and they will combine their energies, whereas at other points a peak will coincide with a trough and they will cancel each other out – hence the light and dark 'interference fringes'.

Michelson proposed to transmit the interfering beams at right angles to each other and have them reflected back and recombined near the source. Now let us imagine that the orientation of the whole apparatus is at such an angle to the aether wind that the velocity of light along the two paths is equal (see figure 2.2). Imagine yourself looking at the interference fringes. Now imagine that the whole apparatus is rotated with respect to the aether wind so that the velocity of light becomes faster along one path and slower along the other (see figure 2.3). Then, considering just one path for a moment, what was once the point where a *peak* impinged might no longer be such a point. The same applies to the other half of the beam. The

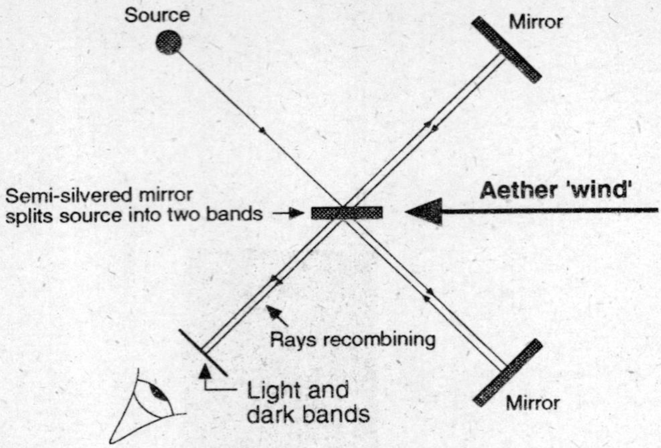

Figure 2.2. Velocity of light equal along both paths.

effect would be that the points of reinforcement and cancelling would shift; that is, that the dark and light bands would be displaced sideways.

In this experimental design, to detect the movement of the earth through the aether there is no need to know which way the aether wind blows at the outset of the experiment, all one needs to do is to rotate the instrument and look for shifts in the fringes. It is possible to calculate both speed and direction once one knows the full range of movement of the fringes.

The above explanation glosses over a very serious point. In Michelson's apparatus the light rays were sent out along a path and then reflected back. Thus, if they were swept along fast with the aether in one direction, they would be slowed in the other; it seems as though the effect would cancel out. Well, the arithmetic shows that this is not quite true. The gain is not completely cancelled by the loss, but it does mean that the effect is very much smaller than it would be if there was a way to recombine the beams without bringing them back to the starting point – which there is not. Effectively this means that, instead of looking for a change in the velocity of light of about 1 in 10 000, one is reduced to looking for an effect in the region of 1 in 100 000 000. It is, then, a very delicate experiment indeed. Neverthe-

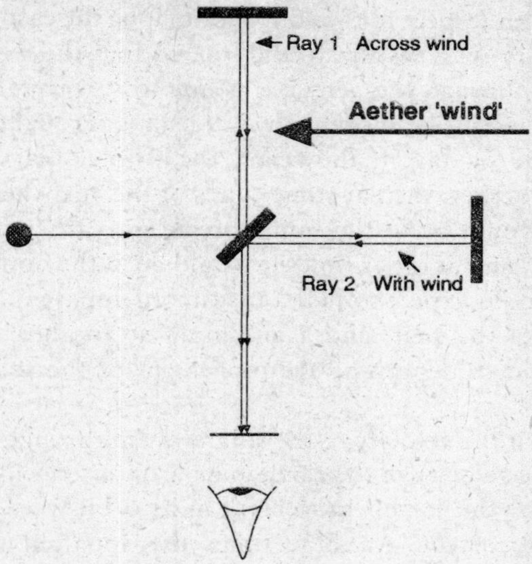

Figure 2.3. One path across aether wind; one path with aether wind.

less, as he developed his apparatus, Michelson expected to see the fringes move about four tenths of the width of a single fringe if the aether wind blew at a speed equal to the earth's velocity in its orbit. This he ought easily to observe.

The elements of the experiment

It is important to note that the apparent velocity of the aether wind would depend on the orientation of the apparatus, and this would change as the earth rotated on its axis; sometimes the wind would seem to blow along the light paths, and sometimes upwards or downwards through the apparatus, when it would have little differential effect on the two light paths. Thus the experiment had to be repeated at different times of the day while the earth rotated so that different orientations could be tested. Further, to understand the movement fully it would be necessary to repeat the experiment at various times of the year when the earth would be moving in different directions with respect to the sun. Should it be the case that the aether was stationary with respect to the sun, so that the whole movement of the earth through the aether was due to its orbital velocity, then the velocity would be more or less constant throughout the year at any one time of day. If, however, the whole solar system moved through the aether, then at some times of the year the earth's orbital movement would be in the same direction as the movement of the solar system, and at other times it would be in the opposite direction. Thus one would expect to find a maximum apparent 'wind speed' at one season of the year, and a minimum at another. The difference could be used to determine the movement of the solar system as a whole.

Note that if the velocity of the solar system through the aether was similar to the velocity of the earth in its orbit, there would be times of the year when the earth's movement in its orbit would nearly cancel the sun's movement. At these times the apparent velocity of the aether wind would be very low or even zero. This would be an unlikely coincidence, but to rule it out it was necessary to make observations during two seasons of the year.

For the experiment to work, the path lengths of the light rays had to be kept constant so that they would be affected only by changes in the direction of the aether wind. The apparent changes in length that were to be observed were of the order of a single wavelength of light. Since the path lengths were of the order of tens of metres, and the wavelengths of visible light is measured in units of a thousand millionths of a metre, it was hard to keep the apparatus stable enough. A slight flexing of one of the arms that supported the mirrors would be more than sufficient to throw the readings out. Michelson was to find that a mass of 30 grams placed on the end of one of the arms of an apparatus weighing tons was enough to upset the results dramatically. As for temperature, it was estimated that differential changes as small as 1/100 of a degree would produce an apparent effect three times that to be expected from the aether wind itself. Magnetic effects on the material of the apparatus caused by surrounding metal or the earth's magnetic field might be sufficient to wreck the results in designs where the iron or steel was used to give rigidity, whereas slight changes in humidity could vitiate those experiments where attempts were made to keep paths stable with wooden distance pieces. The need for temperature and vibration control indicated that the experimental apparatus be heavily built on massive foundations in the cellars of strong, well insulated buildings.

Unfortunately, massive apparatus and careful insulation created an opposite problem. It was thought that the aether might be 'dragged' along by massive opaque materials. Thus it could be argued that a well-insulated room at or below ground level in a large building would comprise, in effect, an aether trap; it would be stagnant pool around which the aether breeze wafted. Worse, hills or mountains, or the surface of the earth itself might carry the aether along with them, just as they carry the air. This way of looking at things indicated that the experiment ought to be performed outside, on top of a high mountain, or at least within a light building, preferably made of glass.

There are, then, six elements in the experiment:

1. the light rays must be split and reflected along paths at right angles;
2. observations of fringes must be made at a number of points as the whole apparatus is rotated on its axis;
3. the observations must be repeated at different times of the day to take account of the earth's rotation on its axis;
4. the observations must be repeated at different seasons to take account of the earth's changing direction of movement with respect to the solar system;
5. the experiment, it might be argued, should be carried out in a light, open, or transparent building;
6. likewise, the experiment should be carried out on a high hill or mountain.

The experimental apparatus

Michelson conducted a first experiment in 1881 and, with the collaboration of Arthur Morley, a second and much more refined observation in 1887. In essence the experiment is simple; a beam is split into two, reflected along two paths at right angles, recombined near the source, and the fringes observed. The apparatus is rotated and the observations are repeated, shifts in the position of the fringes being noted. The practice was to observe the position of the fringes at sixteen different positions while the apparatus was rotated through a complete circle. In practice, the experiment was delicate in the extreme. Of his first apparatus, which was built in Germany, Michelson reported great difficulty with vibration. The experiment had to be moved from Berlin to the more peaceful town of Potsdam, and even then the fringes could be made to disappear by stamping on the ground 100 metres from the laboratory. The experimental runs had to be made at night, during periods when there were few external disturbances. The first apparatus had comparatively short path lengths. In subsequent experiments the path lengths were increased by multiple reflection back and forth, thus increasing the sensitivity to the aether wind, but inevitably increasing the sensitivity to vibration and other disturbances too.

The long history of the experiment can be seen, then, as comprising increases in the path length of the two beams, changes in the materials from which the various parts of the apparatus were made, and changes in the location and housing of the experiment.

The 1881 experiment

Michelson's first experiment had a path length of about 120 cm. According to his calculations, an aether wind having something in the region of the earth's orbital velocity would give rise to a displacement of about a tenth of the width of a fringe as the apparatus turned. Michelson felt he would be able to observe this easily if it were there. In building and using this instrument he discovered the problems of vibration and the distortions produced in the arms when the apparatus was rotated about its axis. Nevertheless, he published the results of his observations, which were that no movement of the earth through the aether could be detected.

After publication, the experiment was re-analysed by H. A. Lorentz, who pointed out that in his analysis Michelson had neglected to take account of the non-zero effect of the wind on the transverse arm of the apparatus; even if you row across a current, it will take longer to get there and back than if there is no current at all! When this effect is taken into account, it halves the expected displacement of the fringes. Michelson concluded that, given the difficulties of the original observation and this new estimate for the displacement, it might be that the effect of the expected aether wind was masked in experimental 'noise'. This led him to design and build an improved apparatus.

The Michelson–Morley 1887 experiment

The next apparatus was much more elaborate. It was built at Michelson's home university in Cleveland. A cast iron trough of mercury rested upon brick foundations in a basement room. A massive block of sandstone, about 5 feet square and 14 inches thick, floated on the mercury. It could be set in motion by hand, and once started it would turn slowly so as to complete a full turn in about 6 minutes and would continue to turn on its own for more than hour. The light, beam splitter, reflectors, and so forth were mounted on the sandstone block. A number of mirrors were mounted so as to reflect the beams back and forth several times before they were recombined on the screen. This gave a path length of over 10 metres, and an expected displacement of about four tenths of a fringe as the apparatus rotated.

After the usual trials and tribulations, Michelson and Morley were ready to observe. At noon on 8, 9 and 11 July, and at around 6 pm on 8, 9 and 12 July, Michelson walked round with the rotating apparatus calling out results while Morley recorded the observations. They were deeply disappointed, for no effect remotely resembling the expected speed of the aether wind was found. Once more, the experiment produced a null result.

Now, we remarked above that there are six components in the experiment: transmission at right angles, rotation of the apparatus, observations at different times of day, observation at different times of year, lightweight buildings and an elevated site. What we have described covers only three of the six elements. Michelson seems to have been so disappointed at the result that instead of continuing he immediately set about working on a different problem: the use of the wavelength of light as an absolute measure of length.

The only way one can understand this is to see the experiment through Michelson's eyes, as an earth speedometer. In that case, it would be expected that the speed would be fairly high and that only by a remarkable coincidence – the cancelling of the velocity of the solar system by the equal and opposite velocity of the earth at the time of the experiment – would a low value result. One also has to assume that he was not concerned with the problem of aether 'drag'. The interferometer, as Michelson had built it, was not much use as a speedometer, that much was clear. If, on the other hand, the experiment is thought of as we think of it now – a test of the theory of relativity – its theoretical significance is greater, but its experimental significance is much less. To be a test of relativity, the experiment needs to demonstrate not that the earth is not moving with anything like the expected velocity, but that there is absolutely no difference in the velocity of light in whichever direction it is measured. In the first case, the results were sufficiently disappointing to make it not worthwhile to develop the speedometer further. As a test of relativity, however, the slightest apparent shift in the fringes would be of great moment. And, it would be of enormous importance to try the test at different times of the year because a slight difference in reading at different seasons would have significance for the theory. The 1887 experiment was not, then, a very good test of relativity, even though it was adequate as a test of what Michelson and Morley wanted to know. Only after Einstein's famous papers were published in the first years of the twentieth century did the experiment become 'retrospectively reconstructed' as a famous and decisive proof of relativity.

Morley and Miller in the 1900s

In spite of Michelson's own lack of interest in his findings, discussion did not cease. The results were seen as a 'cloud' in the otherwise clear sky of physics. Numerous explanations were put forward in an attempt to show how the existence of an aether was compatible with the null results. These ranged from new sources of inaccuracy in the experiment, such as errors introduced by movement of the observer's eye, to the 'Lorentz contraction' – the suggestion that matter, including the arms of the interferometer, would shorten in the direction of movement to just the right degree to cancel out the effect. The interest was such that by the early 1900s Morley, and Dayton C. Miller, who had succeeded Michelson as a teacher in the university, were building new and improved interferometers. They built an enlarged device, based on wood, to look for differences in the contraction effect, but found results no different from the metal and sandstone instruments.

Still unsettled was the idea that the aether was trapped, or dragged along, by the dense surroundings of the experiment; the next step was to try the apparatus on high ground. In 1905 Morley and Miller tried the experiment in a glass hut atop a 300 foot hill. They again found what could only be counted as a null result when compared with what might be expected from the earth's orbital velocity.

As they completed this work, Einstein's papers were becoming recognised for what they were and setting the scene for the reinterpretation of the 'null' result as one of the most significant findings of experimental physics. It should not be thought, however, that Einstein's ideas were uniformly accepted upon their publication. The battle lasted several decades. Relativity was resisted for many reasons and on many fronts. There was interest in continued re-examinations of the Michelson–Morley result until beyond the end of the Second World War.

Miller claims to have found an aether drift: his 1920s experiments

As the interferometer experiments came to be seen as tests of relativity, rather than measures of the velocity of the earth, what had been done appeared less than complete. Dayton Miller, partly as a result of encouragement from Einstein and Lorentz, decided to test the results with an apparatus built on top of Mount Wilson, at a height of 6000 feet. When the results of the earlier experiments were examined closely in the context of relativity, they revealed their ambiguity. There was a small effect in the earlier experiments, though the fringe displacement was about one hundredth of a fringe rather than the expected four tenths. For relativity, of course, any real effect, however small, was crucial.

In the early 1920s Miller conducted a number of inconclusive experiments on Mount Wilson, experiencing the usual troubles with temperature control, lack of rigidity of the apparatus, and so forth.

He rebuilt the apparatus and took readings again on 4, 5 and 6 September 1924. Miller now found a persistent positive displacement, and concluded that 'the effects were shown to be real and systematic, beyond any further question'.

Miller's experiment was different from the others in that he pressed ahead with the fourth part of the protocol and took further readings in spring, summer and the following autumn. He concluded, in 1925, that he had found an observed motion of the earth of about 10 kilometres per second – around one third of the result that the original Michelson experiments were expected to find. In 1925, Miller was awarded the 'American Association for the Advancement of Science' prize for this work.

Thus, although the famous Michelson–Morley experiment of 1887 is regularly taken as the first, if inadvertent, proof of relativity, in 1925, a more refined and complete version of the experiment was widely hailed as, effectively, disproving relativity. This experiment was not conducted by a crank or charlatan. It was conducted by one of Michelson's closest collaborators, with the encouragement of Einstein, and it was awarded a major honour in the scientific community.

The initial experimental responses to Miller

There were a number of experimental responses to Miller's finding, all of them claiming a null result. The biggest effort was that made by Michelson himself. He built a huge interferometer and ran it in an insulated laboratory, again with null results. He and Miller confronted each other at a scientific meeting in 1928 and agreed to differ. An elaborate German experiment was also completed at about the same time, and this too found no significant effect. Both of these experiments, it must be pointed out, were well shielded, and neither was conducted at significant elevation. The results of these two experiments seem to have quieted the renewed speculation brought on by Miller's positive results even though they were not carried out under conditions favourable for the recognition of an aether wind. A further experiment was flown from a balloon, solving the altitude problem, but necessitating heavy shielding. As is often the case in science, a 'critical mass' of clearly expressed experimental voices can outweigh the objections of a critic however carefully argued.

In 1930 Michelson's huge device was installed at the top of Mount Wilson, in a telescope housing. The housing was made of metal and was, therefore, more of a potential shield than the housings of Miller's Mount Wilson experiments. In any case, nothing seems to have emerged from these Mount Wilson observations. What is more, although Michelson's interferometer was supposed to be made of 'Invar', an alloy not subject to expansion due to heat, a later analysis showed that the material was not properly formulated.

Miller's 1933 paper and the most recent experiments

In 1933 Miller published a paper reviewing the field and concluding that the evidence for an aether wind was still strong. We have then a classic situation of so-called replication in physics. Miller claimed a positive result, critics claimed negative results, but Miller was able to show that the conditions under which the negative experiments were conducted were not the same as the conditions of his own experiment. In particular, his was the only experiment that was done at altitude and with a minimum of the kind of shielding that might prevent the aether wind blowing past the test apparatus. Miller argued:

> In three of the four [negative] experiments, the interferometers have been enclosed in heavy, sealed metal housings and also have been located in basement rooms in the interior of heavy buildings and below the level of the ground; in the experiment of Piccard and Stahel [an interferometer carried aloft in a balloon], a metal vacuum chamber alone was used . . . If the question of an entrained ether is involved in the investigation, it would seem that such massive and opaque shielding is not justifiable. The experiment is designed to detect a very minute effect on the velocity of light, to be impressed upon the light through the ether itself, and it would seem to be essential that there should be the least possible obstruction between the free ether and the light path in the interferometer. . . .

> In none of these other experiments have the observations been of such extent and of such continuity as to determine the exact nature of the diurnal [due to rotation of earth], and seasonal variation.
>
> *(Miller, 1933, p. 240).*

In spite of this, the argument in physics was over. Other tests of relativity, including the Eddington observations of 1919 (to be discussed below), indirectly bolstered the idea that the theory of relativity was correct and that the velocity of light must be constant in all directions. The sheer momentum of the new way in which physics was done – the culture of life in the physics community – meant that Miller's experimental results were irrelevant.

We have travelled a long way from the notion that the Michelson–Morley experiment proved the theory of relativity. We have reached the point where the theory of relativity had rendered the Michelson–Morley experiment important as a sustaining myth, rather than as a set of results. Results that ran counter to what it was believed the Michelson–Morley experiment demonstrated were largely ignored. Think of it this way. The notion of 'anomaly' is used in science in two ways. It is used to describe a nuisance – 'We'll ignore that; it's just an anomaly', and to signify serious trouble – 'There are some troublesome anomalies in the existing theory.' The interferometry results started as serious trouble for the theory of the aether. The null results passed from anomaly to 'finding' as the theory of relativity gained adherents. With Miller's positive claims, interferometry results became, once more, an anomaly, but this time they were treated as a nuisance rather than a trouble. Miller's results were 'just an anomaly that needed to be explained away'. Miller could not change the status of his positive readings from nuisance to troublesome anomaly even though they were the outcome of the best experiment yet completed, perhaps the only one which could truly be said to have tested what it was meant to test. The meaning of an experimental result does not, then, depend only upon the care with which it is designed and carried out, it depends upon what people are ready to believe.

Postscript

There are, in the scientific community, some with tidy minds who feel uncomfortable even about the anomalies which most think of as merely a nuisance. As late as 1955 a team were re-analysing the whole history of the experiments in an attempt to reconcile Miller's findings with what everyone believed. They concluded that Miller's work had been confounded by temperature changes. Repetitions of the experiment continued after this date. In 1963, experiments were done with a 'maser', the forerunner of the laser, to try to settle the experimental issue. Though, as has been explained, all this was in a sense irrelevant to relativity, it is not irrelevant to the thesis being argued here. Michelson and Morley could not have *proved* relativity, because as late as 1963 the results of the experiments, considered on their own, outside the context of the rest of physics, were not yet clear.

PART 2. ARE THE STARS DISPLACED IN THE HEAVENS?

> The gravitational field of the earth is, of course, too weak for the bending of light rays in it to be proved directly, by experiment. But the famous experiments performed during the solar eclipses show, conclusively though indirectly, the influence of a gravitational field on the path of a light ray.
>
> *(Albert Einstein and Leopold Infeld,* The Evolution of Physics: From Early Concepts to Relativity and Quanta, *New York: Simon and Schuster, 1938, p. 221).*

The curious interrelation of theory, prediction and observation

The general theory of relativity is a complicated business. It is said that even by 1919 there were only two people who fully understood it: Einstein and Eddington. (This, let us hasten to add, is based on a quip of Eddington's.) Even to this day, theorists are not completely united about what follows from Einstein's theory, while in 1919 there was still substantial argument about what exactly should be expected. It was agreed, however, that according to both Newton and Einstein's theories, a strong gravitational field should have an effect on light rays, but that the Einsteinian effect should be greater than the Newtonian effect. The problem was to find out which theory was correct.

The gravitational field of the earth is far too small to have a measurable effect on light, but the sun's field is much greater. The light coming from the stars should be bent as the rays pass through the sun's gravitational field. To us, it should appear that stars close to the sun are slightly displaced from their usual position. The displacement would be greater in the world according to Einstein than in the world according to Newton. Einstein argued that the stars should appear to be shifted twice as much according to his theory as Newton's theory would suggest, though the shifts in either case were very small. It is as though a star whose light grazed the edge of the sun would appear to be displaced by a distance equivalent to the width of a penny viewed from a mile away. In figures, the expected displacements were 0.8 second of arc and about 1.7 seconds of arc for the two theories, a second being 1/3600 of a degree. The apparent movements that were actually observed would, however, be smaller – about half of these – since no stars could be observed that were closer than two solar diameters from the edge.

Einstein's theoretical derivation of the maximum apparent deflection of light rays is, from a modern point of view, somewhat problematic. At the time it 'caused confusion among those less adept than he at getting the right answer' (Earman and Glymour, 1980, p. 55). As in so many delicate experiments, the derivations, though unclear at the time, came to be seen to be correct *after* the observations had 'verified' Einstein's prediction. Science does not really proceed by having clearly stated theoretical predictions which are then verified or falsified. Rather, the validity given to theoretical derivations is intimately tied up with our ability to make measurements. Theory and measurement go hand-in-hand in a much more subtle way than is usually evident.

It is worth dwelling on the subtle co-operation of theory and experiment. Einstein had said that Newton's theory implied, let us say, a deflection of 'N' and his own theory implied a deflection of 'E'. Others (for what we would now agree were good reasons) were not sure that the 'N' and the 'E' were the right implications of the two theories. One would imagine that one could only test which of the two theories was correct after one was certain about the implications of each of them. To take an extreme example, if, in reality, it were the other way round, and Newton's theory implied deflection 'E' while Einstein's implied deflection 'N', measurements of the displacement of the stars, however accurate, would be in danger of confirming the wrong theory. One has to separate the *theory* from the *prediction* 'derived' from that theory. In the event, Eddington obtained measurements that concurred with Einstein's derived prediction, but the results were taken as confirming not only the prediction but also Einstein's *theory*. In interpreting the observations this way, Eddington seemed to confirm not only Einstein's prediction about the actual displacement, but also *his method of deriving the prediction from his theory* – something that no experiment can do.

The logic of this historical process would seem eminently reasonable under certain circumstances. For example, if Einstein's prediction for the deflection had been very exact, and Eddington's observations had been equally exact, and they had matched Einstein precisely, then the coincidence would force one to agree that Einstein must have been 'on to something' even if neither he nor anyone else was completely sure about the derivation of the displacement. But Eddington's observations, like many measurements in science, were not like this. As we shall see, they were very inexact and some of them conflicted with others. When he chose which observations to count as data, and which to count as 'noise', that is, when he chose which to keep and which to discard, Eddington had Einstein's prediction very much in mind. Therefore Eddington could only claim to have confirmed Einstein because he used Einstein's derivation in deciding what his observations really were, while Einstein's derivations only became accepted because Eddington's observation seemed to confirm them. Observation and prediction were linked in a circle of mutual confirmation rather than being independent of each other as we would expect according to the conventional idea of an experimental test. The proper description, then, is that there was 'agreement to agree' rather than that there was a theory, then a test, then a confirmation. When we describe Eddington's observations we will see just how much he needed Einstein's theory in order to know what his observations were.

The nature of the experiment

What has to be done is to compare the position of stars in the open sky with their apparent position when their starlight grazes the edge of the sun. The stars cannot normally be seen when they are close to the sun, or even when the sun is in the sky, because the sun is so bright. Stars can be seen close to the sun only during a solar eclipse. The size of the displacement – Newtonian or Einsteinian – is so small that the only possible chance of measuring it is by comparing photographs of a region of sky with and without the sun present. For the crucial observations one must await a total eclipse, but the comparison photographs must be taken several months before or after, when the sun is absent from that region of the sky. Clearly, the eclipse photographs must be taken during the daytime, but the comparison photographs must be taken at night, the only time (other than during an eclipse) when the stars can be seen.

In an experiment of such delicacy, it is important that as much as possible is kept constant between the observations and the background comparisons. The trouble is that the observation photographs and the comparison plates have to be obtained at different seasons of the year. This means that lots of other things have time to change. Furthermore, observation plates made in the daytime will use a warm telescope, while at night, the camera looks through a cold telescope. The difference in focal length between a hot and a cold telescope will disturb the apparent position of the stars to a degree which is comparable with the effect that is to be measured. There are many other changes, some calculable, some guessable, some unknown, between observation and comparison due to various sources of mechanical strain on the telescope which will minutely change the focal length and the relationship of the photographic plate to the axis of the telescope.

What makes matters worse is that eclipses can usually be seen only from remote corners of the world. It is not possible to take major telescopes, with all their controlling mechanisms, to such locations. The telescopes, therefore, will be relatively small, with relatively low light-gathering power. This means that exposures have to be long – in this case they were in the region of 5–30 seconds – so as to gather enough starlight to produce well-defined images. Long exposures bring with them another range of problems. Not only does the telescope have to be held steady, but it has to be moved to compensate for the rotation of the earth. Major astronomical telescopes are built with complex and finely engineered mounts to rotate the telescope smoothly with respect to the earth so that it is always directed at the same point in the heavens. Mounts of this sort could not be shipped and set up in the remote locations in which the observations were to be made. Instead the images were kept steady by means of 'coleostats', mechanisms based on a moving mirror controlled by a falling weight which reflects light into the telescope. The coleostat mirrors were a further source of distortion, as were their controlling mechanisms.

On top of all these problems, there are, of course, the contingencies of the weather. If clouds cover the sky then all the preparations are wasted. Earlier expeditions had been thwarted by weather (others had been thwarted by the outbreak of the First World War), and in this case clouds limited the value of at least one of Eddington's telescopes though it did not prevent its use entirely.

The scientists, fortunately, were not completely helpless in the face of these difficulties. The photographs of the field of stars contained some stars that were near the sun and others that were distant. According to the theory, distant stars should suffer no displacement. The effect on the telescope of changed focal length, and so forth, should show up as an apparent displacement of the 'undisplaced' stars. Thus it ought to be possible to measure these unwanted effects and compensate for them in the calculations for the 'truly displaced' stars. It turns out that to control for all the known spurious effects there must be at least six 'undisplaced' stars in the frame. But even this part of the experiment is subject to error. The estimation of the spurious effects depends on assumptions about the statistical distribution of errors in the plates. One can now understand that the Eddington observations were not just a matter of looking through a telescope and seeing a displacement; they rested on a complex foundation of assumptions, calculations, and interpolations from two sets of photographs. And this is the case even if the photographs are clear and sharp – which they were not.

The expeditions and their observations

The Eddington observations were actually made by two separate parties, one with two telescopes, the other party with one. The two parties went to two different locations. In March of 1918, A. Crommelin and C. Davidson set sail to Sobral, in Brazil, while Eddington and his assistant, E. Cottingham went to an island off the coast of West Africa called Principe. The Sobral party took with them an 'astrographic telescope' and a 4-inch telescope. This group obtained 19 plates from the astrographic telescope and 8 from the 4-inch telescope during the course of the eclipse, though one of the 4-inch plates was obscured by cloud.

The Principe group had one astrographic instrument with them. The day of the eclipse proved cloudy but, taking their photographs anyway, they obtained 16 plates. Only two of these, each showing only five stars, were usable. Both groups took comparison photographs a few months later, at the same site in the case of the Sobral group, and back at Oxford in the case of the Eddington party.

The best photographs, though they were not completely in focus, were those taken by the Sobral 4-inch telescope. From these plates and their comparisons, Crommelin and Davidson calculated that the deflection of starlight at the edge of the sun would be between 1.86 and 2.1 seconds of arc (the range being obtained by a calculation of 'probable error'), compared with the Einstein prediction of 1.7 seconds. Though the astrographic plates were less satisfactory, the Sobral party were able to make calculations based on 18 of them and obtained a mean estimate of 0.86 seconds, compared with the Newtonian value of 0.84 (probable error bands were not reported for this instrument). Thus, in very broad terms, one of the Sobral instruments supported the Newtonian theory, while the other leaned towards Einstein's prediction for his own theory. The support for the latter was, however, muddied by the fact that the 4-inch telescope gave a result unequivocally too high and the support for Newton was problematic because the photographs from the astrographic telescope were poor.

The two plates from the Principe expedition were the worst of all. Nevertheless, Eddington obtained a result from these plates using a complex technique that *assumed* a value for the gravitational effect.

At first he used a value half-way between Einstein's and Newton's and then repeated the procedure using Einstein's figures. It was not clear what difference these assumptions made though it is worth noting that, in Eddington's method, Einstein's derivation played a part even in the initial calculation of the apparent displacement. From his two poor plates Eddington calculated that the displacement at the edge of the sun would be between 1.31 and 1.91 seconds.

We can convert the 'probable error' calculations of the two groups into the modern langauge of 'standard deviations', and interpolate a standard deviation for the Sobral astrographic. For the Sobral observations the standard deviations are 0.178 for the good plates and 0.48 for the astrographic, while in the case of Eddington's plates the standard deviation is 0.444. (These are the calculations of John Earman and Clark Glymour.) A modern treatment would suggest that, assuming the measurement errors were distributed randomly, there is a 10% chance that the true answer lies further from the mean measurement than 1.5 standard deviations either side. With this in mind, let us sum up what we have so far, giving the 1.5 standard deviation intervals:

10% Confidence intervals for the observations at Sobral and Principe

	Low bound	Mean	High bound
Sobral			
8 good plates	1.713	1.98	2.247
18 poor plates	0.140	0.86	1.580
Principe			
2 poor plates	0.944	1.62	2.276

If we forget about the theory and the derivations, and pretend that we are making measurements in ignorance of the hypothesis – which is, after all, what we do when we do 'double blind testing' for the effectiveness of drugs or whatever – what would we conclude? We might argue that the two sets of poor plates cancel each other out, and that the remaining evidence showed that the displacement was higher than 1.7. Or, we might say that the eight good plates from Sobral were compatible with a displacement from just above 1.7 seconds to just below 2.3, Eddington's two poor plates were compatible with shifts from just above 0.9 to just below 2.3, while the poor Sobral plates were compatible with shifts from near zero to just below 1.6. In either case, it would be difficult to be able to provide a clear answer. Nevertheless, on 6 November 1919, the Astronomer Royal announced that the observations had confirmed Einstein's theory.

Interpretation of the results

Even to have the results bear upon the question it had to be established that there were only three horses in the race: no deflection, the Newtonian deflection, or the Einsteinian deflection. If other possible displacements had been present in the 'hypothesis space' then the evidence would be likely to give stronger confirmation to one or other of them. For example, if the displacement were hypothesised to be around 2 seconds, then the best readings – the Sobral 4-inch – could be said to confirm this result. There were other contenders at the time, but the rhetoric of the debate excluded them and presented the test as deciding between only the three possibilities: 0.0, 0.8 and 1.7.

Now let all the other horses in the race be scratched at the post. Do the results come down on Einstein's side in an unambiguous way? The answer is that they do not. To make the observations come out to support Einstein, Eddington and the others took the Sobral 4-inch results as the main finding and used the two Principe plates as supporting evidence while ignoring the 18 plates taken by the Sobral astrographic. In the debate which followed the Astronomer Royal's announcement, it appears that issues of authority were much to the fore. On 6 November 1919, Sir Joseph Thomson, the President of the Royal Society, chaired a meeting at which he remarked: 'It is difficult for the audience to weigh fully the meaning of the figures that have been put before us, but the Astronomer Royal and Professor Eddington have studied the material carefully, and they regard the evidence as decisively in favour of the larger value for the displacement' (quoted in Earman and Glymour, 1980, p. 77).

In 1923, however, an American commentator, W. Campbell, wrote:

> Professor Eddington was inclined to assign considerable weight to the African determination, but, as the few images on his small number of astrographic plates were not so good as those on the astrographic plates secured in Brazil, and the results from the latter were given almost negligible weight, the logic of the situation does not seem entirely clear.
>
> *(Quoted in Earman and Glymour, 1980, p. 78).*

Eddington justified ignoring the Sobral astrographic results by claiming that they suffered from 'systematic error' – that is, some problem that meant that the errors were not randomised around the mean but that each reading was shifted systematically to a lower value. If this was true of the Sobral astrographic and not true of the other two sets of readings, then Eddington would have been quite justified in treating the results as he did. It appears, however, that at the time he was unable to educe any convincing evidence to show that this was the case.

In the end, Eddington won the day by writing the standard works which described the expeditions and their meaning. In these he ignored the 18 plates from the Sobral astrographic and simply described the 1.98 result from the 4-inch and the 1.671 result from his own two plates. When one has these two figures alone to compare with a Newtonian prediction of around 0.8 and an Einsteinian prediction of around 1.7, the conclusion is inevitable. But there was nothing inevitable about the observations themselves until Eddington, the Astronomer Royal, and the rest of the scientific community had finished with their after-the-fact determinations of what the observations were to be taken to be. Quite simply, they had to decide which observations to keep and which to throw out in order that it could be said that the observations had given rise to any numbers at all.

Ten more eclipse observations were conducted between 1922 and 1952. Only one, in 1929, managed to observe a star that was closer than two solar radii from the edge of the sun, and this suggested that the displacement at the edge would be 2.24 seconds of arc. Most of the other nine results were also on the high side. Although there are other reasons to believe the Einstein value, the evidence on the bending of visible star light by the sun, at least up to 1952, was either indecisive or indicated too high a value to agree with the theory. And yet 1919 remains a key date in the story of relativity. Is this because science needs decisive moments of proof to maintain its heroic image?

CONCLUSION TO PARTS 1 AND 2

None of this is to say that Einstein was wrong, or that the eclipse experiments were not a fascinating and dramatic element in the great change which our understanding of nature has undergone in the twentieth century. But we should know just what the experiments were like. The picture of a quasi-logical deduction of a prediction, followed by a straightforward observational test is simply wrong. What we have seen are the theoretical and experimental contributions to a cultural change, a change which was just as much a licence for observing the world in a certain way as a consequence of those observations.

The way that the 1919 observations fit with the Michelson–Morley experiment should be clear. They were mutually reinforcing. Relativity gained ground by explaining the Michelson–Morley anomaly. Because relativity was strong, it seemed the natural template through which to interpret the 1919 observations. Because these observations then supported relativity further, the template was still more constraining when it came to dealing with Miller's 1925 observations.

While all this was going on, there were still other tests of relativity that had the same mutually reinforcing relationship to these tests as they had to each other. For example, there were observations of the 'red-shift'. It followed from Einstein's theory that light coming from the sun should be affected by the sun's own gravitational field in such a way that all wavelengths would be shifted slightly toward the red end of the spectrum. The derivations of the quantitative predictions were beset with even more difficulties than the calculations of the bending of light rays. The experimental observations, conducted both before and after 1919, were even more inconclusive. Yet after the interpretation of the eclipse observations had come firmly down on the side of Einstein, scientists suddenly began to see confirmation of the red-shift prediction where before they had seen only confusion. Just as in the example of gravitational radiation discussed in chapter 5, the statement of a firm conclusion elicited firm grounds for reaching that conclusion. Once the seed crystal has been offered up, the crystallisation of the new scientific culture happens at breathtaking speed. Doubt about the red-shift turned into certainty. John Earman and Clark Glymour, from whom we have borrowed much of our account of the Eddington observations, put it this way:

> There had always been a few spectral lines that could be regarded as shifted as much as Einstein required; all that was necessary to establish the red-shift prediction was a willingness to throw out most of the evidence and the ingenuity to contrive arguments that would justify doing so. The eclipse results gave solar spectroscopists the will. Before 1919 no one claimed to have obtained spectral shifts of the required size; but within a year of the announcement of the eclipse results several researchers reported finding the Einstein effect. The red-shift was confirmed because reputable people agreed to throw out a good part of the observations. They did so in part because they believed the theory; and they believed the theory, again at least in part, because they believed the British eclipse expeditions had confirmed it. Now the eclipse expeditions confirmed the theory only if part of the observations were thrown out and the discrepancies in the remainder ignored . . . *(Earman and Glymour, 1980, p. 85).*

Thus, Eddington and the Astronomer Royal did their own throwing out and ignoring of discrepancies, which in turn licensed another set of ignoring and throwing out of discrepancies, which led to conclusions about the red-shift that justified the first set of throwing out still further. What applies in the relationship in any two of these sets of observations applies, *a fortiori* to all the tests of relativity that were taking place around the same time. No test viewed on its own was decisive or clear cut, but taken together they acted as an overwhelming movement. Thus was the culture of science changed into what we now count as the truth about space, time and gravity. Compare this process with, say, political direction of scientific consensus from the centre – which is close to what once happened in the Soviet Union – and it is admirably 'scientific', for the scientists enter freely into their consensual position, leaving only a small minority of those who will not agree. Compare it, however, to the idealised notion of scientific 'method' in which blind tests prevent the observer's biasses entering into the observations, and it is much more like politics.

We have no reason to think that relativity is anything but the truth – and a very beautiful, delightful and astonishing truth it is – but it is a truth which came into being as a result of decisions about how we should live our scientific lives, and how we should licence our scientific observations; it was a truth brought about by agreement to agree about new things. It was not a truth forced on us by the inexorable logic of a set of crucial experiments.

Appendix to chapter 2 part 2

In history, as in science, facts do not speak for themselves – at least not exactly. The interpretation that Professors Earman and Glymour would put on their data might not entirely match the conclusion of this book. It is because Earman and Glymour cleave to rather different views of the nature of science than we do that we have been particularly careful to stay close to their account. We have popularised and clarified wherever we can but we have done our best to avoid any possibility of seeming to distort their material.

The section of this chapter which is most close to Earman and Glymour's original starts at the sub-heading 'The nature of the experiment', and finishes around page 51 at the paragraph which ends with the sentence: 'It appears, however, that at the time he was unable to educe any convincing evidence to show that this was the case'. In other places, other sources, and more of our own interpretation creep in.

It is, perhaps, only fair to Earman and Glymour to quote their own conclusion:

> This curious sequence of reasons might be cause enough for despair on the part of those who see in science a model of objectivity and rationality. That mood should be lightened by the reflection that the theory in which Eddington placed his faith because he thought it

> beautiful and profound – and, possibly, because he thought that it would be best for the world if it were true – this theory, so far as we know, still holds the truth about space, time and gravity. (p. 85).

Appropriately understood, we ourselves see no reason to disagree with this.

3

The sun in a test tube: the story of cold fusion

When two chemists working at the University of Utah announced to the world's press on 23 March 1989 that they had discovered fusion, the controlled power of the hydrogen bomb, in a test tube, they launched the equivalent of a scientific gold rush. And the gold was to be found everywhere – at least in any well-equipped laboratory. The two scientists were Martin Fleischmann and Stanley Pons.

The apparatus was simple enough (see figure 3.1): a beaker of heavy water (like ordinary water but with the hydrogen atoms replaced by 'heavy hydrogen', otherwise known as deuterium); a palladium 'electrode' known as the cathode, and a platinum electrode, known as the anode. A small amount of the 'salt', lithium-deuteroxide, was added to the heavy water to serve as a conductor. Though these substances are not in everyday use, and are rather expensive, they are quite familiar to any modern scientist; there is nothing exotic about the apparatus. Put a low voltage across this 'cell' for a period of up to several hundred hours, and out should come the gold: fusion power. The heavy hydrogen atoms should fuse together into helium, releasing energy; this is the way the sun is powered. The telltale signs of fusion were heat and nuclear byproducts such as neutrons – sub-atomic particles – and traces of the super-heavy hydrogen atom, tritium.

Pons and Fleischmann added an intriguing tease to the account of their success. They warned that the experiment was only to be attempted on a small scale. An earlier cell had mysteriously exploded

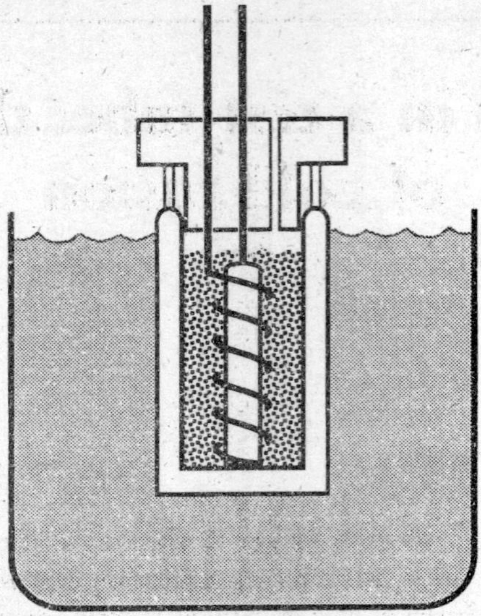

Figure 3.1. Cold fusion cell (redrawn by Steven W. Allison from Close, 1991, p.76).

vaporising the palladium and producing a large hole in the concrete floor of the laboratory. Luckily it had happened during the night and no-one was hurt.

The experiment seemed straightforward and there were plenty of scientists willing to try it. Many did. It was wonderful to have a simple laboratory experiment on fusion to try after the decades of embarrassing attempts to control hot fusion. This effort required multi-billion dollar machines whose every success seemed to be capped with an unanticipated failure. 'Cold fusion' seemed to provide, as Martin Fleischmann said during the course of that famous Utah press conference, 'another route' – the route of little science.

Scientists the world over immediately started scrambling for information about the experiment. Details were hard to come by. Faxes, electronic mail networks, newspapers and television all played a role. Some scientists did not wait for details. That same night enterprising students at MIT started the first attempted replications based on a video of a television news programme on which the apparatus had briefly been shown. Such experiments had little chance of success because the exact conditions employed by Pons and Fleischmann were not yet known. Like the worm-running experiments discussed in chapter 1, cold fusion experiments were to suffer from their apparent simplicity – at least in the early days before scientists recognised just how complicated a palladium–deuterium electrolytic cell could be. Within a week a photocopied manuscript showing the technical details of the experiment became available. Now replication started with a vengeance. Scarce supplies of palladium were bought up and pieces of equipment were scavenged from everywhere. Many stayed up all night nursing their electrolytic cells. Science had seen nothing like it; neither had the world's press which ran continuous news items and updates of progress. It was 'science by press conference' as scientists queued up to announce their latest findings and predictions to the media.

And for a while it looked as if cold fusion was real. Amazingly, in the week following the first announcement it became clear that there was not just one Utah cold fusion group, but two. The second independent group was located at nearby Brigham Young University and they too had been getting positive results for the previous three years. This group, headed by physicist Steven Jones, had not found excess heat, but had detected neutrons from a cold fusion cell (although at a much lower level than claimed by Pons and Fleischmann). Both groups had submitted their results to the prestigious scientific journal *Nature*.

Texas A&M University soon announced to the waiting media that they too were seeing excess heat from a cold fusion cell, and then came an announcement from Georgia Tech that they were seeing neutrons. Positive results were reported from Hungary and elsewhere in Eastern Europe. Rumours of positive results came in from all over the scientific world. The Japanese were supposed to be launching their own massive detection programme.

Patents had been filed on behalf of Pons and Fleischmann by the University of Utah. Indeed part of the reason for the press release before the results were published in a scientific paper (a breach of scientific etiquette which was to be held against the scientists) was the University of Utah's concern to ensure priority over the nearby group at Brigham Young University. Utah seemed set to become the Gold Rush State with the State Legislature meeting and voting $5 million towards the cold fusion effort. Congress was approached for a possible further $25 million. Even President Bush was being kept appraised of developments.

But then doubts started to surface. It transpired that Georgia Tech had made a mistake; their neutron detector turned out to be heat sensitive. The Texas A&M excess heat measurements were explained away by an improperly earthed temperature sensitive device. Groups at MIT and national laboratories such as Lawrence Livermore and Oak Ridge were not yet seeing anything. Pons and Fleischmann's paper was mysteriously withdrawn from *Nature*. Congress decided to put the $25 million on hold.

At the American Physical Society meeting that May in Baltimore, with the ever-present media circus in attendance, criticism reached a crescendo. An MIT group claimed that Pons and Fleischmann had incorrectly interpreted their evidence for neutrons; a prestigious California Institute of Technology (Cal Tech) group reported detailed replication attempts, all negative, and cast doubt upon the correctness of the Utah measurements of excess heat; and finally a Cal Tech theorist pronounced that cold fusion was impossible theoretically and accused Pons and Fleischmann of delusion and incompetence. The University of Utah pair were not at the meeting to defend themselves, but Steven Jones from the other Utah cold fusion group was there. Unfortunately, even Jones distanced himself from Pons and Fleischmann's work, claiming that he too had doubts about the measurements of excess heat.

For most of the gathered community of physicists, already sceptical about whether chemists could overturn cherished assumptions about fusion physics, enough was enough. Gold became fool's gold, or that at least is how the story goes. As we shall see, like most of the episodes examined in this book, there is more to be said; much more.

The little science route to fusion

One can chart the rise and decline of cold fusion from the price of palladium. On 23 March, 1989, just before the announcement of the discovery, the price was $145.60 an ounce. By May 1989 at the height of the cold fusion frenzy the price had risen to $170.00 an ounce. Prices plummeted following the Baltimore APS meeting. As of today (October 1992) the price has fallen back to $95.00 an ounce.

It is palladium, or rather one property of palladium, which provided the impetus to the search for cold fusion. It is known that palladium has a surprising ability to absorb vast quantities of hydrogen. If a piece of palladium is 'charged' with as much hydrogen as it can absorb, then the pressure inside the crystal lattice dramatically increases. Perhaps at such high pressures the normal barrier of positive charge (known as the Coulomb barrier) preventing nuclei coming together to fuse could be overcome. It was a long-shot but scientists before Pons and Fleischmann had actually tried to produce fusion between hydrogen nuclei this way.

In the 1920s, soon after the discovery of the atomic structure of matter, two German chemists working at the University of Berlin attempted to produce fusion of hydrogen using palladium. Fritz Paneth and Kurt Peters were not interested in fusion as a source of energy but in the product, helium, which was used in airships. New ways to make helium were urgently sought by German industry because the USA, the main commercial supplier, refused to sell helium to Germany after the First World War. Paneth and Peters, knowing of palladium's affinity for hydrogen, set up an experiment in which they passed hydrogen over red-hot palladium. They claimed to detect the presence of small amounts of helium. Unfortunately they later discovered that the probable source of the helium was gas already absorbed in the glass walls of their apparatus. However, their work was taken up another scientist and inventor: John Tandberg, a Swede who worked at the Electrolux Corporation Laboratory in Stockholm.

Tandberg had remarkably similar ideas to those of Pons and Fleischmann 60 years later, or so it seems with hindsight. In 1927 he had applied for a patent for a device to manufacture helium by the electrolysis of water with a palladium cathode. In his device hydrogen produced at the cathode entered the palladium lattice and there, with the huge pressures induced by absorption, underwent fusion to produce helium. That at least was the claim. The only substantial difference between Tandberg's device and the later set-up of Pons and

Fleischmann was the use of light water as the electrolyte. Tandberg's patent was rejected because the description was said to be too sketchy. However, after the discovery of deuterium (in the 1930s) Tandberg pursued the work further by attempting to create fusion in a wire of palladium which had been saturated with deuterium by electrolysis. It seems he met with little success, at least in regard to the production of helium.

Pons and Fleischmann were unaware of the earlier work when they started their experiments in 1984. Martin Fleischmann is one of Britain's most distinguished electrochemists. Stanley Pons (an American), visited the University of Southampton to study for his PhD in 1975 and that is where the two met. Fleischmann, who was Faraday Professor of Electrochemistry at Southampton, had a reputation for being the sort of scientist who liked to carry out high-risk science, pursuing bold and innovative ideas and approaches. Indeed he had built his career with such work and some of the risks had paid off. Fleischmann had made a number of important discoveries, as recognised by his election as a Fellow of the Royal Society in 1986.

The reason for Fleischmann being in Utah in 1989 had to do with British Prime Minister, Margaret Thatcher. The Thatcher cutbacks of funding to British universities in 1983 meant that Fleischmann was forced to take early retirement from the University of Southampton (where he retained an un-paid position). He became a freelance researcher teaming up with Pons who was by now a productive scientist in his own right, and chair of the University of Utah Chemistry Department. Pons was aged 46 and Fleischmann 62 when the discovery was announced. Pons, too, had a reputation for successful high-risk science. Pons and Fleischmann were well aware that cold fusion was a long-shot. They initially funded experiments with $100 000 of their own money, expecting to see at most tiny traces of tritium and perhaps some neutrons. The levels of excess heat they detected were a complete surprise.

Jones' involvement

The announcement of 23 March 1989 cannot be understood without reference to the work of the other Utah group, led by Steven Jones at

Brigham Young University. While the scientific community were unfamiliar with Pons and Fleischmann's work on cold fusion, they had been following Jones' progress for several years. In 1982 Jones and his colleagues had undertaken a major experimental effort looking for fusion triggered by sub-atomic particles produced at the Los Alamos particle accelerator. They had found far more evidence of such fusions than theory would have led them to expect, but not enough to make a source of viable energy. Like hot fusion research, particle-induced fusion was a frustrating step away from the excess energy output needed for commercial exploitation.

Jones had moved on to consider how very high pressures might encourage hydrogen isotopes to fuse. The key breakthrough in his thinking came in 1985 when Brigham Young geophysicist Paul Palmer drew his attention to the anomaly of excess heavy helium (helium-three) found near volcanoes. Palmer and Jones thought this could be explained by deuterium contained in ordinary water undergoing geologically induced cold fusion inside the earth.

The Brigham Young group pursued the idea, attempting to reproduce the geological processes in the laboratory. They were searching for a metal, traces of which in rock might serve as a catalyst for fusion. They built an electrolytic cell essentially similar to that of Tandberg and tried various materials for the electrodes. Soon they too decided that palladium, with its ability to absorb hydrogen, was the most likely candidate. The group built a low-level neutron detector to measure any fusion which was occurring. In 1986 they started to observe neutrons at a rate just above background levels. By 1988, using an improved detector, they felt confident that they had found definite evidence of neutron production.

Jones had carried out this research unaware of the similar efforts being carried out at the nearby University of Utah. He first heard of Pons and Fleischmann's experiments in September 1988 when he was sent their research proposal to referee by the Department of Energy (Pons and Fleischmann had at last decided that their work merited funding from public sources).

It was unfortunate for both groups that such similar work was being pursued in such close proximity. In view of the obvious commercial payoff which might result from cold fusion and the need for patent protection it meant that a certain amount of rivalry and suspicion arose between the two groups. Exactly what they agreed regarding the joint publication of their results is still disputed.

It seems that in early 1989 Pons and Fleischmann were hoping that Jones would hold off from publishing for a period (up to eighteen months), giving time for them to refine their measurements. Pons and Fleischmann were, it appears, confident that they were seeing excess heat, but had no firm evidence for its nuclear origins. Some crude measurements indicated that neutrons were coming out, but more exact measurements were desirable. Fleischmann even tried to arrange to have a cold fusion cell flown out to the Harwell Laboratory in England where he was a consultant and where very sensitive neutron detectors were available. Unfortunately the cell was declared a radiation risk and could not be taken across international boundaries. In the event Pons and Fleischmann claimed they could indirectly detect neutrons by observing interactions in a water shield surrounding the cell. It was these hastily carried out measurements which were later to be challenged by the MIT group; they turned out to be the Achilles heel in the Utah body.

Pons and Fleischmann were under pressure from Jones' impending announcement. Although Jones cancelled one seminar in March, he planned to announce his results at the meeting of the American Physical Society on 1 May. Pons and Fleischmann, in order not to lose their priority claim, reached an agreement with Jones to dispatch separate papers from both groups to *Nature* on 24 March.

In March, however, communication between the two groups broke down. Although Jones was going to speak in May his abstract was made public beforehand. Pons and Fleischmann, it seems, took this as licence to go public themselves. Also, the University of Utah group were worried that Jones might be stealing their ideas on excess heat, having had access to their work via the Department of Energy research proposal. A further complicating factor was a request in March to Pons from the editor of the *Journal of Electroanalytical Chemistry* for a paper on his latest work. Pons quickly wrote up an account of the cold fusion experiments which he submitted to the journal. It was this paper (published in April 1989), which would eventually be widely circulated, and provided the first technical details of the experiments.

Under growing pressure from the Utah administration, Pons and

Fleischmann decided to go ahead with a press conference on 23 March, the day before the planned joint submission to *Nature*. A leak from Fleischmann to a British journalist meant that the first report of the discovery appeared in the British *Financial Times* on the morning of 23 March. Thus the world's press were primed to descend on Utah. At the press conference no mention was made of the other Utah group.

Jones, who was by now infuriated both by the press conference and the revelation that a paper had already been submitted, considered the agreement to have been broken and immediately dispatched his own paper to *Nature*. Nothing could be more symbolic of the mis-communication which had arisen between the two Utah groups than the lone figure of Marvin Hawkins (a graduate student who worked with Pons and Fleischmann), waiting at the Federal Express office at Salt Lake City Airport at the appointed hour on 24 March for someone from Jones' group to appear. No-one arrived and the Pons and Fleischmann paper was mailed alone.

The controversy

It was Pons and Fleischmann's results that gave rise to the cold fusion controversy. The levels of neutrons detected by Jones were of lower orders of magnitude and he has never claimed to observe excess heat. Jones' results also did not pose the same theoretical challenge. Furthermore, Jones, unlike Pons and Fleischmann, made a point of playing down the commercial application angle.

The detrimental effect on the credibility of scientists' findings when they get caught up in a scientific controversy not of their own choosing is revealed by the reception of Jones' results. Few would doubt, given his previously established reputation in the field, the minimal theoretical consequences his results posed, and the modest manner in which he presented them, that, if it had not been for Pons and Fleischmann, Steve Jones would by now have quietly established an interesting fact about the natural world: fusion of small amounts of deuterium in palladium metal.

Despite his attempts to distance himself from the other Utah group, Jones has inevitably been subject to the same suspicions. The reality of his neutron measurements has come into question, and there is no consensus as to whether he has observed fusion.

Pons and Fleischmann, unlike Jones, had no established reputation in the field of fusion research; they were chemists not physicists. Moreover they were claiming something which to most physicists was theoretically impossible. Not only did it seem extremely unlikely that fusion could be occurring, but also, if all the heat excess was caused by *fusion*, then the levels of neutrons produced should have been more than enough to have killed Pons and Fleischmann and anyone else who happened to be in the close proximity of one of their cells. In short, fusion could not occur and, if it did, then they should be dead. This is what one might refer to as a 'knockdown' argument!

There is little doubt that when fusion researchers heard the news on 23 March they were sceptical. The reaction was:

'Suppose you were designing jet airplanes and then you suddenly heard on CBS news that somebody had invented an antigravity machine.' (Quoted in Mallove, 1991, p. 41).

Another remarked at the time:

'I'm willing to be open-minded, but it's really inconceivable that there's anything there.' (Ibid., p. 41).

Part of the scepticism came from fusion researchers being only too familiar with grandiose claims for breakthroughs which shortly afterwards turn out to be incorrect. There had been many such episodes in the history of the field and thus fusion scientists were wary of extravagant claims. For them, solving the world's energy problems via a breakthrough in fusion had about as much chance of being true as the perennial claims to have superseded Einstein's theory of relativity.

Though fusion researchers, well-used to spectacular claims, and with their own billion-dollar research programs to protect, were incredulous, other scientists were more willing to take the work seriously. Pons and Fleischmann have fared better with their colleagues in chemistry where, after all, they were acknowledged experts. Early on Pons presented his findings to a meeting of the American Chemical Society where he was given a rapturous reception. For most, the prejudices of the scientific community probably mattered less than the fact that the experiment seemed easy to perform. If there was anything to it, most scientists reckoned, then all should soon become clear. Pons and Fleischmann had two sorts of evidence to back up their claims: excess heat and nuclear products. These had to be tested.

Excess heat

Testing for excess heat was in essence no more than a high-school physics problem. A careful account of the power input and output of the cell was kept, including all the known chemical reactions that are capable of transforming chemical energy into heat. This accounting needs to be carried out over a period of time because at any one moment the books might not balance as energy might get stored in the cell (turning it into a heat bank, as one might say). It is a fairly straightforward procedure to establish the power output by measuring the temperature rise, the cell first having been calibrated using a heater of known power. In practice the experiment took some time to perform because the palladium electrodes had to be fully charged with deuterium (for 8 mm diameter electrodes this could take several months).

The heat excess varied between cells. Some cells showed no heat excess at all. The power sometimes came in surges; in one case four times as much power was recorded coming out as went in. However, more routinely the heat excess was between 10% and 25%.

Despite the capricious nature of the phenomenon, Pons and Fleischmann were confident that the heat excess could not be explained by any known chemical process or reaction.

Nuclear products

The most direct proof of fusion would be the production of neutrons correlated with the excess heat. The first neutron measurements attempted by Pons and Fleischmann were relatively crude. The output from a cell was compared with the background as measured at a distance of 50 metres from the cell. A signal three times the background was recorded for this one cell. This was a suggestive result, but as neither the energy of the neutrons was known, nor whether the background was the same close to the cell as at 50 metres distance, it was far from conclusive. A more satisfactory procedure was to measure the gamma-ray bursts produced by neutrons captured by protons in the water bath surrounding the cell. These measurements were made over a two-day period by Bob Hoffman, a Utah radiologist. The numbers of neutrons detected if any were billions less than would be expected if all the heat was produced by the deuterium fusion reaction.

Another piece of evidence for fusion having taken place would be the presence of its products, such as tritium. Pons and Fleischmann found traces of tritium in the palladium cathode of one cell. The difficulty with this finding – a problem which has beset all the claims – is that tritium is a known contaminant of heavy water.

Replication

As mentioned already, after the announcement on 23 March attempts to repeat the experiments followed fast and furious. Although they got much media attention, these early results (both positive and negative) counted for little. The embarrassment caused by the premature announcements from Georgia Tech and Texas A&M cautioned those scientists who were seriously trying to repeat the experiment that they faced a long struggle. Many were taken in by the seeming ease of the experiment only to discover that a palladium electrolytic cell was a deal more complicated than expected.

Part of the difficulty facing scientists trying to repeat the experiment was that Pons and Fleischmann's account of what they had done was insufficiently detailed. There was discussion of the exact size of the electrodes to be used, the current densities at which to operate the cells, whether the lithium salt was crucial or could be substituted by another salt, whether the cathode was 'poisoned' and with what, and for how long the experiment should run. None of these were clear. Following on from their initial announcement, Pons and Fleischmann were inundated with requests for information. In the frenetic atmosphere at Utah it is no wonder that scientists did not always find it easy to get the crucial information.

Some have accused Pons and Fleischmann of deliberate secrecy in order to secure patent rights or (later on, when many became disillusioned) to hide their own incompetence. However, given the commercial importance of the discovery, securing the patent rights is no small matter; it is routine in areas of biotechnology. Also it seems that Pons and Fleischmann were initially hesitant because of their own uncertainties and their fears about the dangers of the experiment. They were also worried about creating a cheap source of tritium, since tritium is one of the crucial ingredients of a hydrogen bomb.

The elusive details of the experiments were soon spreading through an informal network of electronic mail and telephone contacts. Indeed, electronic mail may have been important in this controversy in producing the rapid consensus against cold fusion which developed after the Baltimore American Physical Society meeting. For instance, Douglas Morrison, a CERN (European Organisation for Nuclear Research) physicist and early enthusiast of cold fusion, set up an electronic newsletter which seems to have been widely read. Morrison soon became sceptical of the claims and referred scientists to Irving Langmuir's notorious talk on 'pathological science', where a number of cases of controversial phenomena (including N-Rays and ESP) in science were dismissed as a product of mass delusion. (Langmuir's talk was reproduced in *Physics Today* in October 1989.) Cold fusion was, according to Morrison, the most recent case of pathological science.

What became clear early on was that, while most groups saw nothing, a few had positive results. The classic problem of replication during a scientific controversy was surfacing. Negative results could be explained away by the believers as being due to differences in the replicating experiment. To those who failed to find anything, however, this was simply confirmation that there was nothing to be found. Fleischmann and Pons's own attitude, as expressed in their testimony to Congress in April 1989, was that they were not surprised by the negative results as many cells were being set up with incorrect parameters and dimensions.

Of the early positive replications reported, one of the most important came from Robert Huggins, a materials scientist at Stanford University. Huggins had run two cells, one with ordinary water and one with heavy water, and found that only the heavy water cell produced excess heat. This answered a long-running criticism of Pons and Fleischmann for not setting up a 'control' cell with ordinary water. Huggins has consistently found positive results over the years.

Another criticism of the Pons and Fleischmann work was that the cells they used were open cells from which the gases produced in electrolysis (deuterium and oxygen) could escape. The worry here was whether the energy balance was affected by the possible chemical recombination of deuterium and oxygen to form heavy water, thereby adding heat to the system. This objection was finally overcome when John Appleby of Texas A&M (*not* the same Texas A&M group which prematurely announced positive results) performed closely controlled calorimetry experiments using closed cells. Heat excesses were again found.

Of the negative results, one of the most influential came from a Cal Tech group headed by chemist Nathan Lewis and physicist Charlie Barnes. The Cal Tech team had tried a variety of combinations of conditions and had found nothing. As mentioned already, Lewis reported the negative results to the Baltimore American Physical Society meeting to dramatic effect. His results had extra impact since he implied that Pons and Fleischmann were guilty of an elementary oversight. They had neglected to stir the electrolyte thus allowing hot spots to develop and produce spurious temperature readings.

However, it seems that Lewis' charges were misplaced. Pons and Fleischmann claimed that there was no need to stir the electrolyte because the deuterium bubbles produced by the reaction did the job sufficiently well. In order to demonstrate the error Lewis had tried to make an exact copy of Pons and Fleischmann's cell. He had taken as his source a photograph of a cell in the *Los Angeles Times*. It turns out that this cell was only used by Pons and Fleischmann for demonstration purposes and was of much larger dimensions than the cells used in actual experimental runs. Pons and Fleischmann were later able to demonstrate with a simple experiment placing a few drops of dye in the electrolyte that the bubbles acted as an adequate stirring mechanism.

As in other controversies what was taken by most people to be a 'knockdown' negative result turns out, on closer examination, to be itself subject to the same kinds of ambiguities as the results it claims to demolish. If Lewis' measurements had been unpacked in the same kind of detail reserved for Pons and Fleischmann they might not have seemed as compelling as they did at the time. In the atmosphere of the Baltimore meeting, where physicists were baying for the blood of the two chemists, and where a whole series of pieces of negative evidence was presented (see below), Lewis was able to deliver the knock-out blow.

The classic problem of replication has surfaced with another set of highly influential negative findings, those reported by Harwell. As a result of Fleischmann's contact with Harwell, David Williams, an ex-graduate student of Fleischmann's, actually started his experiments *before* the March announcement. The results obtained to all intents and purposes killed off cold fusion in Britain. Again on the face of it the experiments look impressive with a number of cells being checked for excess heat and neutrons over lengthy periods.

The results, however, are not compelling for proponents of cold fusion such as Eugene Mallove, who claim that almost half the cells were run at currents below the threshold for cell activity. Other criticisms have been made of the Harwell methods of heat estimation. Despite the differing interpretations of the Harwell experiment, for many scientists it was the last word on cold fusion.

As well as attempts to replicate the phenomenon by setting up electrolytic cells, new experiments have searched for cold fusion by other methods. One such is cooling and reheating the palladium so that it becomes supersaturated with deuterium. Bursts of neutrons have been detected in such experiments.

The difficulty which the proponents face in getting positive results accepted is well illustrated by the fate of the tritium measurements. It will be recalled that Pons and Fleischmann had themselves found traces of tritium. More evidence came from other experimenters, including a group in India with a long history of making tritium measurements, a group at Los Alamos and a third group at Texas A&M University. However, since tritium is a known contaminant of heavy water there is a ready-made 'normal' explanation for all such results. It has proved to be impossible to satisfy the critics that no contamination has occurred, because they can always think of ways in which tritium might get into the cell.

It has even been suggested that the affair has involved fraud. In 1990, an article in the journal *Science* puts forward fraud as a factor in the Texas A&M tritium measurements. The impasse between proponents and critics, an impasse made worse by each side accusing the other of 'unscientific' behaviour, is typical of scientific controversies. The critics cite a preponderance of negative results as grounds to dismiss the controversial phenomenon and any residual positive results are explained away as incompetence, delusion or even fraud. The proponents, on the other hand, account for the negative results as having arisen from the failure to reproduce exactly the same conditions as used to obtain positive results. Experiments alone do not seem capable of settling the issue.

Cold fusion: a theoretical impossibility?

Most of the debate has been fought out against a background in which cold fusion has been held to be impossible on theoretical grounds. Although Pons and Fleischmann, like Tandberg beforehand, hoped that the extreme pressures inside the palladium lattice would help enhance fusion of deuterium, there was little theoretical justification that this would be the case.

One of the responses of nuclear physicists to the cold fusion claims has been a detailed re-examination of the theoretical possibilities. Cal Tech theorist Steve Koonin has devoted considerable time and energy to this problem. Although in reworking the calculations Koonin discovered errors which increased the rate of deuterium–deuterium fusion by a factor of over 10 billion compared with earlier calculations, the main thrust of his work has been to show why deuterium fusion in palladium in the amount needed to produce excess heat is extremely unlikely. Koonin has pointed out that the increased pressure inside palladium was not enough to bring about fusion. Indeed, in a palladium lattice the deuterium nuclei would actually be further apart than in ordinary heavy water. His calculations for the likelihood of deuterium–deuterium fusion showed that the rate would be extremely slow. In a telling comparison Koonin described it this way: 'A mass of cold deuterium the size of the Sun would undergo one fusion per year.'

Thus Koonin, in reviewing all the theoretical possibilities at the May meeting of the American Physical Society, was able to make theoretical justifications seem preposterous. As Koonin told a *New York Times* reporter: 'It is all very well to theorize about how cold fusion in a palladium cathode might take place . . . one could also theorize about how pigs would behave if they had wings. But pigs don't have wings!' (quoted in Mallove, 1991, p. 143).

In a context where the experimental evidence was fast vanishing it was little wonder that most physicists were happy to go along with the accepted wisdom.

There is no doubt that Koonin represents the standard view. As is typical for a scientific controversy where experiment seems to go against prevailing theory, however, there is more to say than this. Indeed throughout the cold fusion episode a number of suggestions have been made as to how fusion might occur on the necessary scale and furthermore how it might occur without neutrons being produced. Some of the more serious suggestions have come from physics Nobel Laureate Julian Schwinger and the MIT laser physicist who helped invent the X-ray laser, Peter Hagelstein. One idea has been to think of ways whereby a rare neutronless fusion reaction could be the source of the excess heat, with energy being transferred into the palladium lattice. Hagelstein, drawing upon ideas in laser physics, has also proposed 'coherent fusion', whereby chains of fusion reactions occur in a kind of domino effect.

With the experimental results under a cloud, most theorists see little reason to entertain such exotic ideas. One is reminded of the solar-neutrino case (see chapter 7), where many speculative theories were produced to explain the discrepancy between standard theory and the experimental results. Even though the discrepancy there was only a matter of a factor of 3 none of the alternative theories gained widespread acceptance. It seems unlikely that, in a case where the discrepancy is a factor of 57 orders of magnitude (10 with 56 0s after it) and where the experimental results have much less credibility, conventional theory is going to be over-thrown. There is no doubt that Hagelstein himself takes these alternative theories very seriously – he has even applied for patents for devices based upon his theories. The risks in pursuing such theories beyond the mere 'what if' stage (i.e. treating such theories as serious candidates rather than mere speculations) are well illustrated by the Hagelstein case: there have been persistent rumours that his tenure at MIT was in jeopardy after he started to produce theoretical explanations of cold fusion.

Credibility

The struggle between proponents and critics in a scientific controversy is always a struggle for credibility. When scientists make claims which are literally 'incredible', as in the cold fusion case, they face an uphill struggle. The problem Pons and Fleischmann had to overcome was that they had credibility as electrochemists but not as nuclear physicists. And it was nuclear physics where their work was likely to have its main impact.

Any claim to observe fusion (especially made in such an immodest and public manner), was bound to tread upon the toes of the nuclear physicists and fusion physicists who had already laid claim to the area. A vast amount of money, expertise, and equipment had already been invested in hot fusion programs and it would be naive to think that this did not affect in some way the reception accorded Pons and Fleischmann.

This is not to say that the fusion physicists simply rejected the claims out of hand (although a few did), or that it was a merely a matter of wanting to maintain billion-dollar investments (although with the Department of Energy threatening to transfer hot fusion funding to cold fusion research there was a direct threat to their interests), or that this was a matter of the blind prejudice of physicists over chemists (although some individuals may have been so prejudiced); it was simply that no scientists could hope to challenge such a powerfully established group without having his or her own credibility put on the line. As might be expected, the challenge to Pons and Fleischmann has been most acute in the area where the physicists feel most at home, the area of the neutron measurements.

Neutron measurements

For many physicists it was the neutron measurements which provided the best evidence for fusion. Yet paradoxically these measurements formed the weakest link in Pons and Fleischmann's claims. As we have seen, the measurements were carried out belatedly and under pressure from others. Worse, neither Pons nor Fleischmann had any special expertise in such measurements.

It was at Harwell, at a seminar given by Fleischmann shortly after the March announcement, that the first inkling of difficulties was to arise. Fleischmann presented the evidence of neutrons and showed a graph of the gamma-ray peak obtained by Hoffman from the water shield. To physicists in the audience who were familiar with such spectra, the peak looked to be at the wrong energy. The peak was at 2.5 MeV whereas the expected peak for gamma-rays produced by neutrons from deuterium should have been at 2.2 MeV. It looked as if something had gone awry with the calibration of the gamma-ray detector, but it was impossible to tell for certain because Fleischmann did not have the raw data with him and had not made the measurements himself. In any event by the time the graph appeared in the *Journal of Electroanalytical Chemistry* the peak was given at the correct value of 2.2 MeV.

Whether the two versions arose from 'fudging' or genuine errors and doubt over what had been measured is unclear. Frank Close, in his much publicised sceptical book about the cold fusion controversy, *Too Hot To Handle*, suggests that the graph was deliberately doctored – a charge taken up by science journalist William Broad in an article in the *New York Times*, of March 17, 1991. Such accusations should, however, be treated with caution. Close, in particular, falls into the trap of exposing all the gory detail of the proponents' experiments, leaving the critics' experiments to appear as clear-cut and decisive. Such a one-sided narrative merely serves to reaffirm the critics' victory.

The neutron measurements soon came under further scrutiny. Richard Petrasso, of the MIT Plasma Fusion Center, also noticed that the shape of the gamma-ray peak looked wrong. The difficulty in taking this observation further was that Pons and Fleischmann had not yet released their background gamma-ray spectrum. What the

MIT scientists did was to pull off something of a scientific scoop. They obtained a video of a news programme which showed the inside of Pons and Fleischmann's laboratory including a VDU display of their gamma-ray spectrum. Petrasso concluded that the claimed peak could not exist at 2.2 MeV and that furthermore it was impossible to see such a slim peak with the particular instrument used. The absence of a Compton edge also eliminated the peak as a viable candidate for neutron capture. The conclusion of the MIT group was that the peak was 'probably an instrumental artefact with no relation to γ-ray interactions'.

Preliminary reports of the work were given by Petrasso at the Baltimore meeting to maximum rhetorical effect. In tandem with the Cal Tech negative results they were to have the decisive impact on the course of the controversy which we have already charted.

The criticism of the neutron measurements was eventually published in *Nature* along with a reply from Pons and Fleischmann. Although they made much of MIT's resort to a news video as a source of scientific evidence (pointing out that what had been referred to by Petrasso as a 'curious structure' was none other than an electronic cursor and denying that the video had shown a real measurement), the Utah pair were now placed on the defensive. They published their full spectrum showing no peak at 2.2 MeV but claiming evidence for a new peak at 2.496 MeV. Although they could not explain this peak in terms of a known deuterium fusion process they maintained the peak was produced by radiation from the cell. In an ingenious move they tried to turn Petrasso's argument around by saying that if indeed their instrument was not capable of detecting such peaks then the lack of a peak at 2.2 MeV should not in itself be taken as evidence against fusion. MIT replied in turn claiming that the peak at 2.496 MeV was actually at 2.8 MeV.

Many scientists have taken this episode as showing that the main argument in favour of fusion had collapsed. However, another interpretation is possible. This is that the best evidence for cold fusion always came from the excess heat measurements – the experimenters' own strength. The hastily performed nuclear measurements had always been puzzling because too few neutrons were observed. In trying to 'come clean' on the difficulties of interpreting their nuclear measurements Pons and Fleischmann were attempting to draw attention back to the main thrust of their argument – the excess heat measurements. Indeed, when Pons and Fleischmann finally published their full results in July 1990, the paper was almost entirely about calorimetry – no nuclear measurements were reported.

The trouble was that for many physicists the nuclear data were what had got them excited in the first place and the weakness of the neutron evidence left the excess heat measurements as mere anomalies, possibly of chemical origin. Furthermore, the problems over the nuclear measurements could easily be taken to demonstrate Pons and Fleischmann's incompetence as experimenters. Despite the Utah pair being widely acknowledged as experts in electrochemistry, this kind of 'guilt by association' seems to have paid off for the critics and has helped discredit the experiment as a whole.

Conclusion

In our account we have focussed mainly on the early stages of the controversy, pointing in particular to the role of the Baltimore American Physical Society meeting where the tide turned against Pons and Fleischmann. Today scientists still continue to work on the phenomenon, some positive results are reported, and conferences are held on such topics as 'Anomalous Phenomena in the Palladium–Deuterium Lattice'. Indeed, the very labelling of the phenomena in this way reflects a feature familiar from other controversies where, in order to try to get the controversial phenomenon accepted, proponents play down its implications for other scientists. Gone are the bold claims that the phenomenon is definitely fusion and gone is the prospect of a new source of commercial energy just around the corner (although Japanese companies continue to invest money). It may eventually be established that there is something unusual going on in the palladium–deuterium lattice but that something is unlikely to be cold fusion as it appeared *circa* March 1989. The failure in 1989 to attract significant Department of Energy funding means that, compared with its initial promise, cold fusion research is in decline. The Utah National Cold Fusion Institute was finally wound up in June 1991.

In the cold fusion controversy the stakes were very high and the normally hidden working of science has been exposed. The cold fusion episode is often taken to show that there is something wrong with modern science. It is said that scientists claimed too much, based on too little, and in front of too many people. Press review is said to have replaced peer review. False hopes of a new age of limitless energy were raised, only to be dashed.

Such an interpretation is unfortunate. Pons and Fleischmann appear to have been no more greedy or publicity seeking than any prudent scientists would be who think they have on their hands a major discovery with a massive commercial payoff. The securing of patents and the fanfare of press conferences are inescapable parts of modern science, where institutional recognition and funding are ever more important. There is no turning the clock back to some mythical Golden Age when scientists were all true gentlemen (they never were anyway, as history of science has taught us in recent years). In cold fusion we find science as normal. It is our image of science which needs changing, not the way science is conducted.

4

The germs of dissent: Louis Pasteur and the origins of life

Spontaneous generation

'Spontaneous generation' is the name given to the doctrine that, under the right circumstances, life can form from dead matter. In a sense, nearly all of us believe in spontaneous generation, because we believe that life grew out of the primeval chemical slime covering the newly formed earth. This, however, is taken to be something that happened slowly, by chance, and once only in the history of the earth; it ought never to be seen in our lifetimes.

The question of the origin of life is, of course, as old as thought but, in the latter half of the nineteenth century, the debate raged within the scientific community. Could new life arise from sterile matter over and over again, in a few minutes or hours? When a flask of nutrients goes mouldy, is it because it has become contaminated with existing life forms which spread and multiply, or is it that life springs anew each time within the rich source of sustenance? It was a controversial issue, especially in nineteenth-century France because it touched upon deeply rooted religious and political sensibilities.

Our modern understanding of biochemistry, biology and the theory of evolution is founded on the idea that, aside from the peculiar conditions of pre-history, life can only arise from life. Like so many of our widespread scientific beliefs we tend to think that the modern view was formed rapidly and decisively; with a few brilliant experiments conducted in the 1860s, Louis Pasteur speedily defeated outright those who believed in spontaneous generation. But the route, though it might have been decisive in the end, was neither speedy nor straightforward. The opposition were crushed by political manoeuvering, by ridicule, and by Pasteur drawing farmers, brewers, and doctors to his cause. As late as 1910, an Englishman, Henry Bastian, believed in the spontaneous generation heresy. He died believing the evidence supported his view.

As in so many other scientific controversies, it was neither facts nor reason, but death and weight of numbers that defeated the minority view; facts and reasons, as always, were ambiguous. Nor should it be thought that it is just a matter of 'those who will not see'. Pasteur's most decisive victory – his defeat of fellow Frenchman Felix Pouchet, a respected naturalist from Rouen, in front of a commission set up by the French Academie des Sciences – rested on the biasses of the members and a great stroke of luck. Only in retrospect can we see how lucky Pasteur was.

The nature of the experiments

The best-known experiments to test spontaneous generation are simple in concept. Flasks of organic substances – milk, yeast water, infusions of hay, or whatever – are first boiled to destroy existing life. The steam drives out the air in the flasks. The flasks are then sealed. If the flasks remained sealed, no new life grows in them – this was uncontested. When air is readmitted, mould grows. Is it that the air contains a vital substance that permits the generation of new life, or is it that the air contains the already living germs – not metaphorical, but literal – of the mould. Pasteur claimed that mould would not grow if the newly admitted air was itself devoid of living organisms. He tried to show that the admission of sterile air to the flasks had no effect; only contaminated air gave rise to putrescence. His opponents claimed that the admission of even pure air was sufficient to allow the putrefaction of the organic fluids.

The elements of the experiment are, then:

1. one must know that the growth medium is sterile but has nutritive value;

2. one must know what happens when the flasks are opened; is sterile air being admitted or is contamination entering too?

Practical answers to the experimental questions

Nowadays we believe we could answer those questions fairly easily, but in the nineteenth century the techniques for determining what was sterile and what was living were being established. Even what counted as life was not yet clear. It was widely accepted that life could not exist for long in a boiling fluid, so that boiling was an adequate means of sterilisation. Clearly, however, the medium could not be boiled dry without destroying its nutritive value. Even where the boiling was more gentle it might be that the 'vegetative force' of the nutrient might have been destroyed along with the living organisms. What counted as sterile air was also unclear. The distribution of micro-organisms in the world around us, and their effect on the air which flowed into the flasks, was unknown.

Pasteur made attempts to observe germs directly. He looked through the microscope at dust filtered from the air and saw egg-like shapes that he took to be germs. But were they living, or were they merely dust? The exact nature of dust could only be established as part of the same process that established the nature of putrescence.

If germs in the air could not be directly observed, what could be used to indicate whether air admitted to a flask was contaminated or not? Air could be passed through caustic potash or through sulphuric acid, it could be heated to a very high temperature or filtered through cotton wool in the attempt to remove from it all traces of life. Experiments in the early and middle part of the nineteenth century, using air passed through acids or alkalis, heated or filtered, were suggestive, but never decisive. Though in most cases admission of air treated in this way did not cause sterilised fluids to corrupt, putrescence occurred in enough cases to allow the spontaneous generation hypothesis to live on. In any case, where the treatment of the air was extreme, it might have been that the vital component which engendered life had been destroyed, rendering the experiment as void as the air.

Air could have been taken from different places – high in the

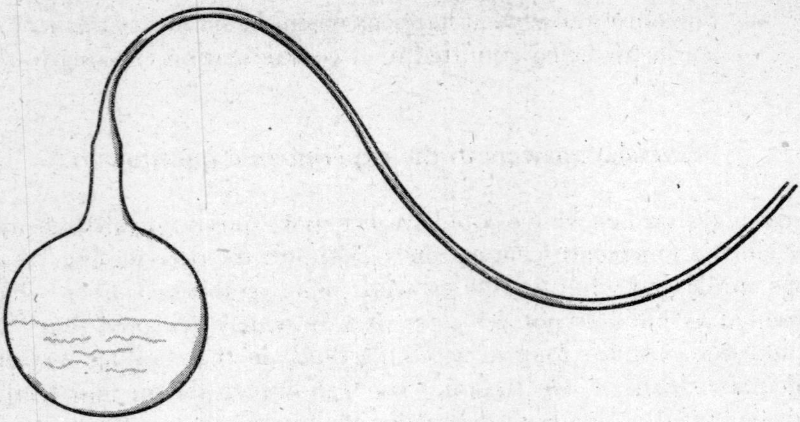

Figure 4.1. One of Pasteur's swan-neck flasks.

mountains, or low, near to cultivated fields – in the expectation that the extent of microbial contamination would differ. To establish the connection between dust and germs, other methods of filtration could be used. Pasteur used 'swan neck flasks' (see figure 4.1). In these the neck was narrowed and bent so that dust entering would be caught on the damp walls of the orifice. Experiments were conducted in the cellars of the Paris Observatoire, because there the air lay sufficiently undisturbed for life-bearing dust to have settled. Later on, the British scientist, William Tyndall, stored air in grease-coated vessels to trap all the dust before admitting it to the presence of putrescible substances. For each apparently definitive result, however, another experimenter would find mould in what should have been a sterile flask. The kinds of arguments that the protagonists would make can be set out on a simple diagram.

Box 1 is the position of those who think they have done experiments that show that life *does* grow in pure air and believe in spontaneous generation. They think these experiments prove their thesis. Box 2 is the position of those who look at the same experiments but do not believe in spontaneous generation; they think there must have been something wrong with the experiment, for example, that the air was not really pure.

Box 4 represents the position of those who think they have done

Possible interpretations of spontaneous generation experiments

		Believe in spontaneous generation	
		Yes	No
Life grows in apparently pure air	Yes	(1) Proves thesis	(2) Air accidentally contaminated
	No	(3) Air spoiled by treatment	(4) Proves thesis

experiments showing that life *does not* grow in pure air and do not believe in spontaneous generation. They think the experiments prove their hypothesis. Box 3 is the position of those who look at the same experiments but do believe in spontaneous generation. They think there must have been something wrong with the air, for example, that its vital properties were destroyed in the purifying process.

There was a period in the 1860s when arguments of the type found in box 3 were important but this phase of the debate was relatively short-lived; it ended as the experimenters ceased to sterilise their air by artificial means and instead sought pure sources of air, or room temperature methods of 'filtration'. Arguments such as those found in box 2 were important for a longer time. They allowed Pasteur virtually to define all air that gave rise to life in the flasks as contaminated, whether he could show it directly or not. This is especially obvious in that part of his debate with Felix Pouchet concerning experiments using mercury, as we shall see.

The Pasteur–Pouchet debate

One episode of the long debate between Pasteur and those who believed in spontaneous generation illustrates clearly many of the themes of this story. In this drama, the elderly (60-year-old) Felix Pouchet appears to serve the role of 'foil' for the young (37-year-old) Pasteur's brilliant role as experimental scientist. Pasteur, there is no doubt, defeated Pouchet in a series of celebrated trials, but the retrospective and triumphalist account glosses over the ambiguities of the trials as they took place in real time.

As with all such experimental controversies, it is the details that are crucial. The argument between Pasteur and Pouchet concerned what happens whan an infusion of hay – 'hay tea', as one might say – which is sterilised by boiling, is exposed to the air. It is undisputed that the infusion goes mouldy – microscopic life forms grow upon its surface – but the usual question remained. Was this because air has life-generating properties or because air contains living 'seeds' of mould?

Experiments 'under mercury'

Pouchet was a believer in spontaneous generation. In his early experiments he prepared sterilised infusions of hay 'under mercury' – to use the jargon. The method was to do the work with all vessels immersed in a mercury trough so that ordinary air could not enter. Specially prepared air could be introduced into the flask by bubbling through the mercury trough. This was the standard way of admitting various experimental gases into experimental spaces without admitting the ordinary air. In Pouchet's case it was purified air that was bubbled through the mercury. It was considered that purified air could be made by heating ordinary air, or by generating oxygen through the decomposition of an oxide; coincidentally this was often mercury oxide which gives off oxygen when heated. Invariably Pouchet found that when purified hay infusions were prepared under mercury, and exposed to pure air, organic life grew. It appeared then that, since all sources of existing life had been eliminated, the new life must have arisen spontaneously.

Pouchet started the debate with Pasteur by writing to him with the results of these experiments. Pasteur wrote back to Pouchet that he could not have been cautious enough in his experiments. "... in your recent experiments you have unwittingly introduced common {contaminated] air, so that the conclusions to which you have come are not founded on facts of irreproachable exactitude' (quoted in Farley and Geison, 1974, p. 19). Here, then, we see Pasteur using an argument of the type that is found in box 2 above. If Pouchet found life when he introduced sterilised air to sterilised hay infusions, then the air *must* have been contaminated.

Later, Pasteur was to claim that, although the hay infusion was sterile in these experiments, and the artificial air was equally devoid of life, it was the mercury that was contaminated with micro-organisms – they were in the dust on the surface of the mercury – and this was the source of the germ.

This is interesting because it seems that the contaminated mercury hypothesis was necessary to explain some of Pasteur's own early results. He reported that in his own attempts to prevent the appearance of life by preparing infusions under mercury, he succeeded in only 10% of his experiments. Though, at the time, he did not know the source of the contamination, he did not accept these results as evidence in support of the spontaneous generation hypothesis. In his own words, he '. . . did not publish these experiments, for the consequences it was necessary to draw from them were too grave for me not to suspect some hidden cause of error in spite of the care I had taken to make them irreproachable' (quoted in Farley and Geison, 1974, p. 31). In other words, Pasteur was so committed in his opposition to spontaneous generation that he preferred to believe there was some unknown flaw in his work than to publish the results. He *defined* experiments that seemed to confirm spontaneous generation as unsuccessful, and vice versa. Later the notion of contaminated mercury replaced the 'unknown flaw'.

Looking back on the incident we must applaud Pasteur's foresight. He was right, of course, and had the courage of his convictions in sufficient degree to refuse to be swayed by what, on the face of it, was a contrary experimental indication. But it *was* foresight. It was not the neutral application of scientific method. If Pasteur, like Pouchet, had been supporting the wrong hypothesis we would now be calling his actions 'dogged obstinacy in the face of the scientific facts'. Perfect hindsight is a dangerous ally in the history of science. We shall not understand the Pasteur–Pouchet debate as it was lived out unless we cut off our backward seeing faculty.

Flasks exposed at altitude

The business of the experiments under mercury was just the preliminary skirmish. The main debate began with Pasteur's experiments on flasks opened to the air at altitude, and Pouchet's rebuttal.

Pasteur prepared flasks with necks drawn out in a flame. He boiled an infusion of yeast and sealed the neck once the air had been driven out. If unopened, the contents would remain unchanged. He could then take the flasks and break the neck at various locations, allowing air to re-enter. To admit air in what ought to be germ-free locations, Pasteur would break the neck with a long pair of pincers which had been heated in a flame, while the flask was held above his head so as to avoid contamination from his clothes. Once the air from the chosen location had entered, Pasteur could once more seal the flask with a flame. Thus he prepared a series of flasks containing yeast infusions together with samples of air taken from different locations. He found that most flasks exposed in ordinary locations became mouldy, whereas those exposed high in the mountains rarely changed. Thus, of 20 flasks exposed at 2000 metres on a glacier in the French Alps, only one was affected.

In 1863, Pouchet challenged this finding. With two collaborators he travelled to the Pyrenees to repeat Pasteur's experiments. In their case, all eight of the flasks exposed at altitude were affected, suggesting that even uncontaminated air was sufficient to begin the life-forming process. Pouchet claimed that he had followed all of Pasteur's precautions, except that he had used a heated file instead of pincers to open the flasks.

Sins of commission

In the highly centralised structure of French science in the mid-nineteenth century, scientific disputes were settled by appointing commissions of the Paris-based Academie des Sciences to decide on the matter. The outcomes of such commissions became the quasi-official view of the French scientific community. Two successive commissions looked into the spontaneous generation controversy. The first, set up before Pouchet's Pyrenean experiments, offered a prize to 'him who by well-conducted experiments throws new light on the question of so-called spontaneous generation'. By accident or design, all members of the commission were unsympathetic to Pouchet's ideas and some announced their conclusions before even examining the entries. Two of its members had already responded negatively to Pouchet's initial experiments and the others were well-known opponents of spontaneous generation. Pouchet withdrew from the competition, leaving Pasteur to receive the prize uncontested for a manuscript he had written in 1861, reporting his famous series of experiments demonstrating that decomposition of a variety of substances arose from air-borne germs.

The second commission was set up in 1864 in response to Pouchet's experiments in the Pyrenees. These experiments had aroused indignation in the Academie, most of whose members had considered the matter to be already settled. The new commission started out by making the challenging statement: 'It is always possible in certain places to take a considerable quantity of air that has not been subjected to any physical or chemical change, and yet such air is insufficient to produce any alteration whatsoever in the most putrescible fluid' (quoted in Dubos, 1960, p. 174). Pouchet and his colleagues took up the challenge adding: 'If a single one of our flasks remains unaltered, we shall loyally acknowledge our defeat' (quoted in Dubos, 1960, p. 174).

The second commission too was composed of members whose views were known to be strongly and uniformly opposed to those of Pouchet. When he discovered its composition, Pouchet and his collaborators attempted to alter the terms of the test. They wanted to expand the scope of the experimental programme while Pasteur insisted that the test should depend narrowly upon whether the smallest quantity of air would always induce putrescence. All Pasteur was required to show, according to the original terms of the competition, was that air could be admitted to some flasks without change to their content. After failing to change the terms of reference, Pouchet withdrew, believing that he would be unable to obtain a fair hearing given the biasses of the members of the commission.

Pouchet's position could not be maintained in the face of his twice withdrawing from competition. That the commissions were entirely one-sided in their views was irrelevant to a scientific community already almost uniformly behind Pasteur.

Retrospect and prospect on the Pasteur–Pouchet debate

Pouchet's position was rather like that of an accused person whose fate hangs on forensic evidence. Granted, the accused was given the chance of producing some evidence of his own, but the interpretation was the monopoly of the 'prosecution' who also acted as judge and jury. It is easy to see why Pouchet withdrew. It is also easy to understand how readily Pasteur could claim that Pouchet's Pyrenean experiments were confounded by his use of a file rather than pincers to cut the neck of the flasks. We can imagine the fragments of glass, somehow contaminated by the file even though it had been heated, falling into the infusion of hay and seeding the nutrients therein. We can imagine that if Pouchet had been forced by the commission to use sterilised pincers after the fashion of Pasteur then many of the flasks would have remained unchanged. We may think, then, that Pouchet's understandable failure of nerve in the face of this technical strait-jacket merely saved him from a greater embarrassment. Although the two commissions were disgracefully biassed, surely this was merely a historical contingency that would not have affected the accurate scientific conclusion they reached?

Interestingly, it now seems that if Pouchet had not lost his nerve he might not have lost the competition. One difference between Pouchet and Pasteur was the nutritive medium they used for their experiments, Pasteur using yeast and Pouchet hay infusions. It was not until 1876 that it was discovered that hay infusions support a spore that is not easily killed by boiling. While the boiling of a yeast infusion will destroy all life, it does not sterilise a hay infusion. Modern commentators, then, have suggested that Pouchet might have been successful if he had stayed the course – albeit for the wrong reasons! It is worth nothing that nowhere do we read of Pasteur repeating Pouchet's work with hay. In fact, except to complain about the use of a file instead of pincers, he hardly ever mentioned the Pyrenean experiments, expending most of his critical energy on the earlier mercury-trough experiments for which he had a ready-made explanation. The Pyrenean experiments, of course, were carried out without mercury, the supposed contaminant in the earlier work. As one of our sources remarks: 'If Pasteur ever did repeat Pouchet's experiments without mercury, he kept the results private' (quoted in Farley and Geison, 1974, p. 33). The conclusion to the debate was reached, then, as though the Pyrenean experiments had never taken place.

The difference between hay and yeast, as we now understand it, adds a piquant irony to the results of the commission. We, however, do not think that Pouchet would have been wiser to go ahead with the challenge, and that scientific facts speak for themselves. The modern interpretation suggests that the facts of hay infusions would have spoken, even to a biassed commission, in the unmistakable voice of spontaneous generation. We don't believe it. The commission would have found a way to explain Pouchet's results away.

Postscript

It is interesting that the defenders of Pasteur were motivated in part by what now seems another scientific heresy. It was thought at the time that Darwinism rested upon the idea of spontaneous generation. In an attack on Darwinism, published in the same year as the second commission was constituted, the secretary of the Academie des Sciences used the failure of spontaneous generation as his main argument. he wrote 'spontaneous generation is no more. M. Pasteur has not only illuminated the question, he has resolved it' (quoted in Farley and Geison, 1974, p. 23). Pasteur, then, was taken to have dealt a final blow to the theory of evolution with the same stroke as he struck down the spontaneous generation of life. One heresy destroyed another. Those who feel that because 'it all came out right in the end', science is vindicated, should think again.

Finally, let us note that we now know of a number of things that might have stopped Pasteur's experiments working if he had pushed them a little further. There are various spores in addition to those found in hay that are resistant to extinction by boiling at 100°C. In the early part of the twentieth century, Henry Bastian was supporting the idea of spontaneous generation by, unknowingly, discovering more of these heat-resistant spores. Further, the dormancy of bacteria depends not only on heat but also on the acidity of the solution. Spores which appear dead in acid solution can give rise to life in an alkaline environment. Thus experiments of the type that formed the basis of this debate can be confounded in many ways. To make sure that a fluid is completely sterile it is necessary to heat it under pressure to a temperature of about 160 °C, and/or subject it to a cycle of heating and cooling repeated several times at the proper intervals. As we now know, there were many ways in which Pasteur's experiments could, and should, have gone wrong. Our best guess must be that they did, but Pasteur knew what he ought to count as a result and what he ought to count as a 'mistake'.

Pasteur was a great scientist but what he did bore little resemblance to the ideal set out in modern texts of scientific method. It is hard to see how he would have brought about the changes in our ideas of the nature of germs if he had been constrained by the sterile model of behaviour which counts, for many, as the model of scientific method.

5

A new window on the universe: the non-detection of gravitational radiation

Detecting gravity waves

In 1969, Professor Joseph Weber, of the University of Maryland, claimed to have found evidence for the existence of large amounts of gravitational radiation coming from space. He used a new type of detector of his own design. The amount of radiation he saw was far greater than the theoretical predictions of astronomers and cosmologists. In the years that followed, scientists tried to test Weber's claims. No-one could confirm them. By 1975, few, if any, scientists believed that Weber's radiation existed in the quantities he said he had found. But, whatever it looks like now, theory and experiment alone did not settle the question of the existence of gravitational radiation.

Gravitational radiation can be thought of as the gravitational equivalent of electromagnetic radiation such as radio waves. Most scientists agree that Einstein's general theory of relativity predicts that moving massive bodies will produce gravity waves. The trouble is that they are so weak that it is very difficult to detect them. For example, no-one has so far suggested a way of generating detectable amounts of gravitational radiation on Earth. Nevertheless, it is now accepted that some sensible proportion of the vast amounts of energy generated in the violent events in the universe should be dissipated in the form of gravitational radiation, and it is this that may be detectable on Earth. Exploding supernovae, black holes and binary stars should produce sizeable fluxes of gravity waves which would show themselves on Earth as a tiny oscillation in the value of 'G' – the constant that is related to the gravitational pull of one object on another. Of course, measuring 'G' is hard enough in itself.

It was a triumph of experimental science when, in 1798, Cavendish measured the gravitational attraction between two massive lead balls. The attractive force between them comprised only one 500 millionth of their weight. Looking for gravitational radiation is unimaginably more difficult than looking for this tiny force because the effect of a gravity wave pulse is no more than a minute fluctuation within the tiny force. To exemplify, one of the smaller gravitational antennae in operation in 1975 (the detectors are often referred to as antennae) was encased in a glass vacuum vessel. The core consisted of, perhaps, 100 kilograms of metal yet the impact of the *light* from a small flashgun on the mass of metal was enough to send the recording trace off scale.

The standard technique for detecting gravitational radiation was pioneered by Weber (pronounced 'Whebber') in the late 1960s. He looked for changes in the length (strains) of a massive aluminium alloy bar caused, effectively, by the changes in gravitational attraction between its parts. Such a bar, often weighing several tons, could not be expected to change its dimensions by more than a fraction of the radius of an atom as a pulse of gravitational radiation passed. Fortunately, the radiation is an oscillation and, if the dimensions of the bar are just right, it will vibrate, or 'ring' like a bell, at the same frequency as the radiation. This means that the energy in the pulse can be built up into something just measurable.

A Weber-bar antenna comprises the heavy bar with some means of measuring its vibrations. Most designs used strain-sensitive 'piezo-electric' crystals glued, or otherwise fixed, to the bar. When these crystals are distorted they produce an electrical potential. In a gravity wave detector the potential produced by the deformation of the crystals is so small as to be almost undetectable. This means that the impulse from the crystals must be amplified if it is to be measured. A critical part of the design is, then, the signal amplifier. Once amplified, the signals can be recorded on a chart recorder, or fed into a computer for immediate analysis.

Such devices don't really detect gravity waves, they detect vibrations in a bar of metal. They cannot distinguish between vibrations

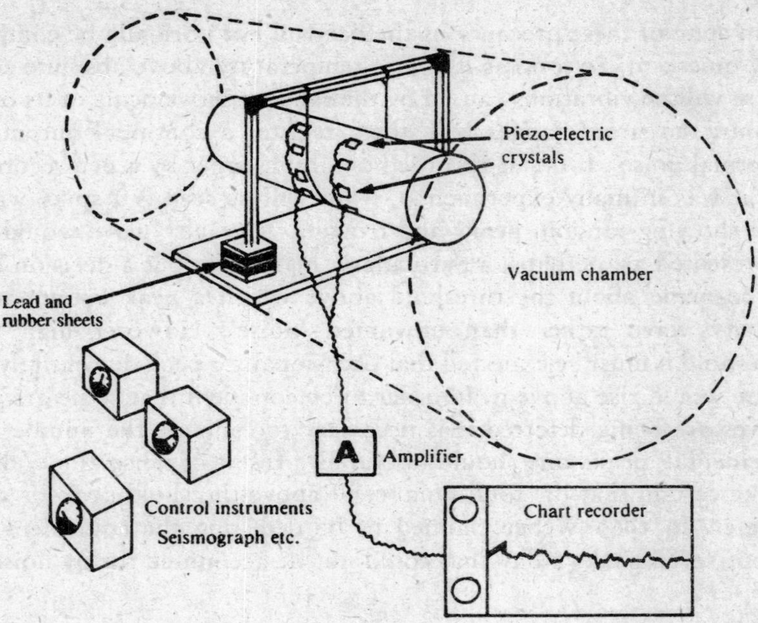

Figure 5.1. Weber-type gravity wave antenna. Compare Weber's method of seismic insulation with the heavy concrete foundations used in the Michelson–Morley experiments (see chapter 2). Heavy foundations actually link the apparatus firmly to the ground thus making certain that vibrations will be channelled through to the apparatus. Remember that Michelson (chapter 2) discovered this his apparatus would be disturbed by stamping on the ground 100 metres from the laboratory. Weber-type detectors are much less sensitive than this due to the ingenious insulation and the narrow waveband of the radiation.

due to gravitational radiation and those produced by other forces. Thus to make a reasonable attempt to detect gravity waves the bar must be insulated from all other known and potential disturbances such as electrical, magnetic, thermal, acoustic and seismic forces. Weber attempted to do this by suspending the bar in a metal vacuum chamber on a thin wire. The suspension was insulated from the ground in an original and effective way by using a stack of lead and rubber sheets.

In spite of these precautions the bar will not normally be completely quiescent. So long as it is at a temperature above absolute zero there will be vibrations caused by the random movements of its own atoms; the strain gauges will, then, register a continual output of 'thermal noise'. If this is recorded on graph paper by a pen recorder (as it was in many experiments), what will be seen is a spiky wavy line showing random peaks and troughs. A gravity wave would be represented as, perhaps, a particularly high peak, but a decision has to be made about the threshold above which a peak counts as a gravity wave rather than unwanted 'noise'. However high the threshold it must be expected that occasionally a peak due entirely to noise would rise above it. In order to be confident that some gravity waves are being detected it is necessary to estimate the number of 'accidental' peaks one should obtain as a result of noise alone, then make certain that the total number of above-threshold peaks is still greater. In 1969 Weber claimed to be detecting the equivalent of about seven peaks a day that could not be accounted for by noise.

Current status of Weber's claims and of gravitational radiation

Weber's claims are now nearly universally disbelieved. Nevertheless the search for gravitational radiation goes on. Weber's findings were sceptically received because he seemed to find far too much gravitational radiation to be compatible with contemporary cosmological theories. If Weber's results were extrapolated, assuming a uniform universe, and assuming that gravitational radiation was not concentrated into the frequency that Weber could best detect, then the amount of energy that was apparently being generated would mean that the cosmos would 'burn away' in a very short time – cosmologically speaking. These calculations suggested that Weber must be wrong by a very long way. The apparatuses now under development are designed to detect the much lower fluxes of radiation that cosmologists believe might be there. The new antennae are 1000 million times more sensitive; they should detect fluxes 1000 million times smaller than Weber said he had found.

Though Weber's first results were not believed because of the amount of radiation he claimed to see, he eventually managed to persuade others to take him more seriously. In the early 1970s he developed his work in a number of ingenious ways, leading other laboratories to attempt to replicate his findings. One of the most important new pieces of evidence was that above-threshold peaks could be detected simultaneously on two or more detectors separated by a thousand miles. At first sight it seemed that only some extra-terrestrial disturbance, such as gravity waves, could be responsible for these simultaneous observations. Another piece of evidence was that Weber discovered peaks in the activity of his detector which happened about every 24 hours. This suggested that the source of the activity had something to do with the rotation of the earth. As the earth rotated, carrying the detector with it, the sensitivity would be expected to vary if the radiation came mostly from one direction in space. The 24 hour periodicity thus indicated that his detectors were being vibrated by an extra-terrestrial source rather than some irrelevant earth-bound disturbance.

What is more, the periodicity at first seemed to relate to the earth's disposition with regard to the galaxy, rather than with regard to the sun – the periodicity related to the astronomical day. This was important, because as the earth moves in orbit round the sun, one would expect the time of day when the detector was most sensitive to change with the seasons. (The geometry is just the same as in the Michelson–Morley experiment; see chapter 2.) This suggested that the source must be outside the solar system – again a strong indicator that it was cosmic events that were causing the gravity wave detector to vibrate rather than something local and uninteresting. This effect became known as the 'sidereal correlation', meaning that the peak periods of activity of the detector were related to the earth's relationship to the stars rather than to the sun.

Persuading others

It is worth noting at this point that with an unexpected claim like Weber's it is necessary to do much more than report experimental results in order to persuade others to take the work sufficiently seriously even to bother to check it! To have any chance of becoming an established result it must first 'escape' from the laboratory of its originator. Persuading other scientists to try to *disprove* a claim is a useful first step. In Weber's case different scientists were convinced by different experimental developments. Some thought one feature was convincing whereas others thought the opposite. For instance, the first of Weber's elaborations was the demonstration of coincident signals from two or more detectors separated by large distances. Some scientists found this convincing. Thus, at the time (1972) one scientist said to Collins:

> [ ] wrote to him specifically asking about quadruple and triple coincidences because this to me is the chief criterion. The chances of three detectors or four detectors going off together is very remote.

On the other hand some scientists believed that the coincidences could quite easily be produced by the electronics, chance, or some other artefact. Thus:

> . . . from talking it turns out that the bar in [ ] and the bar in [ ] didn't have independent electronics at all. . . . There was some very important common contents to both signals. I said . . . no wonder you see coincidences. So all in all I wrote the whole thing off again.

Another elaboration adopted by Weber involved passing the signal from one of the detectors through a time delay before comparing it with the signal from a distant detector. Under these circumstances there should be no coincidences – that is to say, any coincidences would be purely a product of accident. Weber showed that the number of coincident signals did indeed go down when one signal was delayed with respect to the other, suggesting that they were not an artefact of the electronics or a matter of chance. Several scientists made comments such as '. . . the time delay experiment is very convincing', whereas others did not find it so.

Weber's discovery of the correlation of peaks in gravity wave activity with star time was the outstanding fact requiring explanation for some scientists, thus:

> . . . I couldn't care less about the delay line experiment. You could invent other mechanisms which would cause the coincidences to go away . . . The sidereal correlation to me is the only thing of that whole bunch of stuff that makes me stand up and worry about it . . . If that sidereal correlation disappears you can take that whole . . . experiment and stuff it someplace.

Against this, two scientists remarked:

> The thing that finally convinced a lot of us . . . was when he reported that a computer had analysed his data and found the same thing.
>
> The most convincing thing is that he has put it in a computer . . .

But, another said:

> You know he's claimed to have people write computer programmes for him 'hands off'. I don't know what that means. . . . One thing that me and a lot of people are unhappy about, is the way he's analysed the data, and the fact that he's done it in a computer doesn't make that much difference . . .

Picking the right experimental elaboration to convince others requires rhetorical as well as scientific skills.

The experimenter's regress

By 1972 several other laboratories had built or were building antennae to search for gravitational radiation. Three others had been operating long enough by then to be ready to make tentative negative reports. Now we must imagine the problems of a scientist attempting to replicate Weber's experiment. Such a scientist has built a delicate apparatus and watched over it for several months while it generated its yards and yards of chart recorder squiggles. The question is: are there peaks among the squiggles which represent real gravity wave pulses rather than noise? If the answer seems to be 'no' then the next question is whether to publish the results, implying that Weber was wrong and that there are no high fluxes of gravity waves to be found. At this point the experimenter has an agonising decision to make; it could be that there really are gravity waves but the negative experiment is flawed in some way. For example, the decision about the threshold for what counts as real peaks might be wrong, or the amplifier might not be as sensitive as Weber's, or the bar might not be appropriately supported, or the crystals might not be well enough glued to allow the signals to come through. If such is the case, *and* if it turns out that there are high fluxes of gravity waves, then in reporting their non-existence, the scientist will have revealed his own experimental incompetence.

Here the situation is quite unlike that of the school or university student's practical class. The student can have a good idea whether or not he or she has done an experiment competently by referring to the outcome. If the outcome is in the right range, then the experiment has been done about right, but if the outcome is in the wrong range, then something has gone wrong. In real time, the question for difficult science, such as the gravity wave case and the others described in this book, is, '*What is the correct outcome?*'. Clearly, knowledge of the correct outcome cannot provide the answer. Is the correct outcome the detection of gravity waves or the non-detection of gravity waves? Since the existence of gravity waves is the very point at issue, it is impossible to know this at the outset.

Thus, what the correct outcome is depends upon whether there are, or are not, gravity waves hitting the earth in detectable fluxes. To find this out we must build a good gravity wave detector and have a look. But we won't know if we have built a good detector until we have tried it and obtained the correct outcome. But we don't know what the correct outcome is until . . . and so on *ad infinitum*.

This circle can be called the 'experimenter's regress'. Experimental work can only be used as a *test* if some way is found of breaking into the circle of the experimenter's regress. In most science the circle is broken because the appropriate range of outcomes is known at the outset. This provides a universally agreed criterion of experimental quality. Where such a clear criterion is not available, the experimenter's regress can only be avoided by finding some other means of defining the quality of an experiment; and the criterion must be independent of the output of the experiment itself.

Scientists at their work

What should the consequences of the experimenter's regress be? Because no-one knows what counts as the correct result, it is not easy to see who has done a good experiment. We might, then, expect gravity wave scientists to disagree about who had done their experiment well. We might think they would disagree about whether a particular result was the outcome of incompetence on the part of the experimenter and/or flaws in the apparatus. Some scientists would think that Weber saw gravity waves because his methods, or his apparatus, were faulty. Others would think that *failure* to see the radiation must be a consequence of lack of skill, insufficient perseverance, or bad luck. One of the authors of this book, Collins, interviewed most of the scientists involved in the gravity wave work in Britain and America. Such disagreement was precisely what he found. The following set of comments, taken from interviews conducted in 1972, show how scientists' views about others' work varied. In each case, three scientists who come from three different laboratories are commenting on the experiment of a fourth.

Comments on the experiment conducted at W

Scientist (a): . . . that's why the W thing, though it's very complicated, has certain attributes so that if they see something, it's a little more believable . . . They've really put some thought into it . . .

Scientist (b): They hope to get very high sensitivity but I don't believe them frankly. There are more subtle ways round it than brute force . . .

Scientist (c): I think that the group at . . . W . . . are just out of their minds.

Comments on the experiment conducted at X

Scientist (i): . . . he is at a very small place . . . [but] . . . I have looked at his data, and he certainly has some interesting data.

Scientist (ii): I am not really impressed with his experimental capabilities so I would question anything he has done more than I would question other people's.

Scientist (iii): That experiment is a bunch of shit!

Comments on the experiment conducted at Y

Scientist (1): Y's results do seem quite impressive. They are sort of very business-like and look quite authoritative . . .

Scientist (2): My best estimate of his sensitivity, and he and I are good friends . . . is . . . [low] . . . and he has just got no chance [of detecting gravity waves].

Scientist (3): If you do as Y has done and you just give your figures to some . . . [operator] and ask them to work that out, well, you don't know anything. You don't know whether those [operators] were talking to their [friends] at the time.

Comments on the experiment conducted at Z

Scientist (I): Z's experiment is quite interesting, and shouldn't be ruled out just because the . . . group can't repeat it.

Scientist (II): I am very unimpressed with the Z affair.

Scientist (III): Then there's Z. Now the Z thing is an out and out fraud!

Not only do scientists' opinions about the same experiment differ, but every experiment differs from every other in countless ways. Indeed, it is hard to know what it means to do an experiment that is *identical* to another. As one scientist put it:

> Inevitably in an experiment like this there are going to be a lot of negative results when people first go on the air because the effect is that small, any small difference in the apparatus can make a big difference in the observations. . . . I mean when you build an experiment there are lots of things about experiments that are not communicated in articles and so on. There are so called standard techniques, but those techniques, it may be necessary to do them in a certain way.

It is easy, then, to find a difference that will explain and justify a scientist's views about the work of another. Variations in signal processing techniques, in design of the amplifier, in the material of the bar (did it suffer from 'creep'?), in the method of attachment of the piezo-electric crystals, and in many other factors were cited in defence and criticism of the various experiments. Technical arguments, however, were not the only sources of judgement of others' experiments. Other grounds for doubt extended beyond what are usually thought of as science. In 1972, experimenters were casting around for non-technical reasons for believing or disbelieving the results of the various experiments. The list of reasons they provided at the time included the following:

1. Faith in a scientist's experimental capabilities and honesty, based on a previous working partnership.
2. The personality and intelligence of experimenters.
3. A scientist's reputation gained in running a huge lab.
4. Whether or not the scientist worked in industry or academia.
5. A scientist's previous history of failures.
6. 'Inside information'.
7. Scientists' style and presentation of results.
8. Scientists' 'psychological approach' to experiment.
9. The size and prestige of the scientist's university of origin.
10. The scientist's degree of integration into various scientific networks.
11. The scientist's nationality.

As one scientist put it, in explaining why he disbelieved Weber's results:

> You see, all this has very little to do with science. In the end we're going to get down to his experiment and you'll find that I can't pick it apart as carefully as I'd like.

The competence of experimenters and the existence of gravity waves

These arguments over whose work is well done are part and parcel of the debate about whether or not gravity waves exist. When it is decided which are the good experiments, it becomes clear whether those that have detected gravity waves, or those that have not been able to see them, are the good ones. Thus whether gravity waves are there to be detected becomes known. On the other hand, when we know whether gravity waves are there to be detected we know which detectors are good ones. If there are gravity waves a good apparatus is one that detects them; if there are no gravity waves the good experiments are those which do not see them. Thus, defining what counts as a good gravity wave detector, and determining whether gravity waves exist, are the same process. The scientific and the social aspects of this process are inextricable. This is how the experimenter's regress is resolved.

Gravitational radiation: 1975

After 1972, events favoured Weber's claims less and less. In July 1973 negative results were published by two separate groups (two weeks apart), in the scientific journal, *Physical Review Letters*. In December 1973, a third group published negative results in the journal, *Nature*. Further articles claiming that there was nothing to be seen even as the sensitivity of the apparatus was increased were published by these groups and also by three other groups. No-one has since concluded that they found anything that would corroborate Weber's findings.

In 1972, a few scientists believed in the existence of high fluxes of gravity waves, and very few would *openly commit* themselves to their non-existence. By 1975, a number of scientists had spent time and effort actively prosecuting the case against Weber. Most of the others accepted that he was wrong and only one scientist other than Weber thought the search for high fluxes still worth pursuing. One might say that the problem posed by the experimenter's regress had been effectively solved by 1975 – it was now 'known' (by nearly everyone) that an antenna that detected high fluxes of gravity waves was a dud, and one that did not had every chance of being a well-designed experiment. How did this come to pass?

Weber, it seems, was not very surprised at the flood of negative results. A respondent reports that Weber felt that, since a negative result is the easiest thing to achieve, then negative results were to be expected:

> . . . about that time [1972] Weber had visited us and he made the comment, and I think the comment was apt, that 'it's going to be a very hard time in the gravity wave business', because, he felt that he had worked for ten or twelve years to get signals, and it's so much easier to turn on an experiment and if you don't see them, you don't look to find out why you don't see them, you just publish a paper. It's important, and it just says, 'I don't see them'. So he felt that things were going to fall to a low ebb . . .

But it is hard to have complete confidence in an experiment that found nothing. It is hard to see what made scientists so confident that their negative results were correct as long as Weber was still claiming to see gravity waves. Why were they not more cautious? As one scientist remarked:

> ... [a major difference between Weber and the others is that Weber] spends hours and hours of time per day per week per month, living with the apparatus. When you are working with, and trying to get the most out of things you will find that, [for instance] a tube that you've selected, say one out of a hundred, only stays as a good noise tube for a month if you are lucky, but a week's more like it. Something happens, some little grain falls off the cathode and now you have a spot that's noisy, and the procedures for finding this are long and tedious. Meanwhile, your system, to the outside, looks just the same.
>
> So lots of times you can have a system running, and you think it's working fine, and it's not. One of the things that Weber gives his system, that none of the others do, is dedication – personal dedication – as an electrical engineer which most of the other guys are not ...
>
> Weber's an electrical engineer, and a physicist, and if it turns out that he's seeing gravity waves, and the others just missed it, that's the answer, that they weren't really dedicated experimenters ... Living with the apparatus is something that I found is really important. It's sort of like getting to know a person – you can, after a while, tell when your wife is feeling out of sorts even though she doesn't know it.

This feature of experimental work must make scientists wary about drawing clear conclusions from a set of negative results. It is another way of expressing the experimenter's regress. How did they gain enough confidence to damn Weber's findings?

How the debate closed

By 1975 nearly all scientists agreed that Weber's experiment was not adequate but their reasons differed markedly. Some had become convinced because at one point Weber had made a rather glaring error in his computer program; others thought that the error had been satisfactorily corrected before too much damage was done. Some thought that the statistical analyses of the level of background noise and the number of residual peaks was inadequate; others did not think this a decisive point.

Weber had also made an unfortunate mistake when he claimed to have found coincident signals between his own detector and that of an entirely independent laboratory. These coincidences were extracted from the data by comparing sections of tape from the two detectors. Unfortunately for Weber it turned out that because of a confusion over time zones, the two sections of tape he compared had been recorded more than four hours apart so that he was effectively conjuring a signal out of what should have been pure noise. Once more though, it was not hard to find scientists who thought that the damage had not been too great since the level of signal reported was scarcely statistically significant.

Another factor considered important by some was that Weber did not manage to increase the signal-to-noise ratio of his results over the years. It was expected that as he improved his apparatus the signal would get stronger. In fact, the net signal seemed to be going down. This, according to many scientists, was not how new scientific work ought to go. What is more, the correlation with star time that Weber first reported faded away. Again, however, these criticisms were only thought to be decisive by one or two scientists; after all there is no guarantee that a cosmic source of gravity waves should remain stable.

It goes almost without saying that the nearly uniform negative results of other laboratories were an important point. Nevertheless, all of the, roughly, six negative experiments were trenchantly criticised by Weber and, more important, five of them were criticised by one or more of Weber's critics! This should come as no surprise given the analysis in earlier sections of this paper. The one experiment that remained immune to criticism by Weber's critics was designed to be as near as possible a carbon-copy of the original Weber design. No-one thought it was crucial.

What seems to have been most important in the debate was the trenchant criticism, careful analysis, and confrontational style of one powerful member of the physics community Richard Garwin. As one scientist put it:

> ... as far as the scientific community in general is concerned, it's probably Garwin's publication that generally clinched the attitude. But in fact the experiment they did was trivial – it was a tiny thing ... But the thing was, the way they wrote it up ... Everybody else was

> awfully tentative about it ... It was all a bit hesitant ... And then Garwin comes along with this toy. But it's the way he writes it up you see.

Another scientist said:

> Garwin ... talked louder than anyone and he did a very nice job of analysing his data.

And a third:

> [Garwin's paper] ... was done in a very clear manner and they sort of convinced everybody.

When the first negative results were reported in 1972, they were accompanied with a careful exploration of all the logical possibilities of error. Understandably, the first scientists to criticise Weber hedged their bets. Following closely came the outspoken experimental report by Garwin with careful data analysis and the uncompromising claim that the results were 'in substantial conflict with those reported by Weber'. Then, as one respondent put it, 'that started the avalanche and after that nobody saw anything'.

As far as *experimental results* are concerned, the picture that emerges is that the series of negative experiments made strong and confident disgreement with Weber's results openly publishable but that this confidence came only after, what one might call, a 'critical mass' of experimental reports had built up. This mass was 'triggered' by Garwin.

Garwin believed from the beginning that Weber was mistaken. He acted on that belief as he thought proper. Thus he made certain that some of Weber's errors were given wide publicity at a conference and he wrote a 'letter' to a popular physics journal which included the paragraph:

> [it was shown] that in a ... [certain tape] ... nearly all the so-called 'real' coincidences ... were created individually by this single programming error. Thus not only some phenomenon besides gravity waves *could*, but in fact *did*, cause the zero-delay excess coincidence rate [in this data]. [Garwin's stress]

and the statement:

> . . . the Weber group has published no credible evidence at all for their claim of detection of gravitational radiation.

Concerning some of their later work, a member of Garwin's group remarked to me:

> At that point it was not doing physics any longer. It's not clear that it was ever physics, but it certainly wasn't by then.

and

> We just wanted to see if it was possible to stop it immediately without having it drag on for twenty years.

Thus, without the actions of Garwin and his group it is hard to see how the gravity wave controversy would have been brought to a close. That such a contribution was needed is, once more, a consequence of the experimenter's regress.

Conclusion

We have indicated how the experimenter's regress was resolved in the case of gravity waves. The growing weight of negative reports, all of which were indecisive in themselves, were crystallised, as it were, by Garwin. After he had spoken, only experiments yielding negative results were counted and there just were no more high fluxes of gravity waves. All subsequent experiments that produced positive results must, by that very fact, be counted as flawed.

Reporting an experimental result is itself not enough to give credibility to an unusual claim. If such a claim is to be taken sufficiently seriously for other scientists even to try to refute it then it must be presented very clearly and with great ingenuity. Weber had to make a long series of modifications before his claims were given significant notice. Then, once the controversy was under way, a combination of theory and experiment alone was not enough to settle matters; the experimenter's regress stands in the way. We have seen some of the ways in which such issues actually are resolved. These resolving, or 'closure', mechanisms are not normally thought of as 'scientific' activities yet, without them, controversial science cannot work.

It is important to notice that the science of gravity waves after the resolution of the controversy does not look at all like the science of gravity waves before the resolution. *Before* the resolution there was real and substantial uncertainty, and it was very reasonable uncertainty. In spite of the large amount of scientific work that had been done and the large number of experimental and theoretical results that were available, things were not clear. At that point no-one could be blamed for thinking that there were two possibilities open and for being reluctant to plump for one side or the other. *After* the resolution everything is clarified; high fluxes of gravity waves do not exist and it is said that only incompetent scientists think they can see them.

Of course, the model also shows that a controversy once closed may, in principle, be re-opened. Professor Joseph Weber has never ceased to believe that his results were correct and, especially since 1982, after our story ends, has been publishing papers which provide new arguments and evidence in support of his view. The question is, will they gain the attention of the scientific community?

The, pre-resolution, gravity wave science of 1972 is the sort of science that is rarely seen or understood by the science student. Nevertheless, to stress a point that will be made again in the conclusion to the whole book, it is the sort of science that the research scientist may one day face and it is the sort of science that the public are asked to consider when, say, they listen to forensic evidence as members of a jury, or when they attend to public inquiries on technical matters, or when they vote for policies, such as defence or energy policies, which turn on technical matters. For many reasons then, it is as important to understand this unfamiliar face of science as it is to understand its more regular counterpart.

6

The sex life of the whiptail lizard

Introduction

David Crews, a professor of zoology and psychology at the University of Texas, might be thought of as a sexual voyeur. This is because he spends much of his time observing the bizarre sex lives of reptiles such as lizards and snakes. His work is of great interest to biologists. It is sometimes controversial. Our focus in this chapter is on one particular set of observations which Crews made of the mating behaviour of a particular genus of whiptail lizard. However, by way of introduction to the sexual world of reptiles which Crews studies, we will first look at his less controversial work on the red-sided garter snake.

The Arctic environment of western Canada provides perhaps the harshest conditions encountered by any vertebrate on the planet. It is here that the red-sided garter snake lives. In order to survive the long Arctic winter, snakes have learnt the trick of cryopreservation. Their blood becomes extremely thick, and crucial bodily organs stop functioning almost completely, exhibiting barely detectable levels of activity. However, when Spring arrives, they undergo rapid transformation in preparation for mating.

Mating occurs over a short, intense period. The males emerge first from their long winter deep-freeze and spend from three days to three weeks basking in the sun near the entrance to the den. When the females emerge, either alone or in small groups, the males are attracted by a pherome (a messenger substance) on their backs. Up to 100 males converge and form a 'mating ball'. Once a male succeeds in mating, the others immediately disperse. The mated female, who has been rendered unattractive to other males as a result of a pherome which she has received from the mating male, now leaves the locale. The males regroup, waiting by the entrance of the den for the emergence of other females with which to mate.

Why are biologists interested in such a curious ritual? Crews is a behavioural neuroendocrinologist. He studies the evolution of the systems in the body that control reproduction and sexual behaviour. He uses a variety of techniques, including observations of behaviour, examination of organs, and analyses of substances in the blood. Comparisons are made with other species. The garter snake is of particular interest to Crews because of the way that its sexual behaviour and its physiology are synchronised with the demands of the environment. The snakes' sexual activities may seem strange to us, but they have adapted perfectly to the extreme conditions under which they live. For Crews the behaviour of the garter snakes was a particularly powerful illustration of how environmental factors may influence the evolution and development of various aspects of reproduction. By emphasising the role of the environment Crews can be thought of as taking sides in one of the oldest debates in biology: nature versus nurture.

Crews' interest in reproductive physiology is somewhat at odds with the traditional fields of reptile study. His work falls between the interests of herpetologists who study snakes and lizards from a natural history standpoint and neuroendocrinologists who compare various hormonal control systems without necessarily linking their work to the sexual behaviour of the species. With his interest in evolution and in comparing more than one species, Crews also finds audiences for his work among evolutionary theorists, comparative biologists, zoologists and psychologists. Like many scientific innovators, Crews brings together approaches from a variety of areas that traditionally have gone their separate ways. It is partly because of this that his work has been tinged with controversy. By asking new questions of aspects of the behaviour and physiology of species that have already been well studied, Crews was posing a challenge to the established experts.

Of course, just because a scientist's work challenges that of his or her colleagues, does not mean that it will necessarily lend itself to controversy. Many contentious findings or approaches within science are simply ignored. For instance, numerous papers have been published challenging the foundations of quantum mechanics or relativity theory which scarcely cause a ripple on the surface of physics. Turning a blind eye in the no-nonsense way to deal with potentially troublesome ideas. Indeed, obtaining a controversial status for a set of ideas such that other scientists feel compelled to reject them in an explicit manner is a substantial achievement in itself.

By the time Crews produced his controversial work on the whiptail lizard he was too important a figure to ignore. In the early stages of his career at Harvard there was no inkling of the controversy to come. His approach and findings did not challenge the fundamentals of his field. By the time he moved to Texas University (after seven years at Harvard) he was a highly respected, visible, and well-connected scientist. It was only now, after having established himself, that he started to stress the radical quality of his ideas. The most sharply focussed controversy in which Crews has become involved has not centred on the grander issues of evolutionary theory but on some rather specific claims that he made concerning the sexual behaviour of the whiptail lizard. It is his observations of this vertebrate and their reception which form the backbone of our story.

In what follows we shall be particularly concerned to follow the twists and turns of this one scientific controversy. It may seem perverse to go into such detail. However, we would remind the reader that it is exactly in the detailed arguments that we find the rough diamond of science.

'Leapin' lesbian lizards'

This heading was used by *Time* magazine to introduce Crews' observations of the sexual habits of *Cnemidophorus*, the whiptail lizard. *Cnemidophorus* is unusual in the reptile world because it breeds 'parthenogenetically'. That is to say it can reproduce from the eggs of the female without needing a male to fertilise them. This makes the species ideal for studying aspects of the evolution of

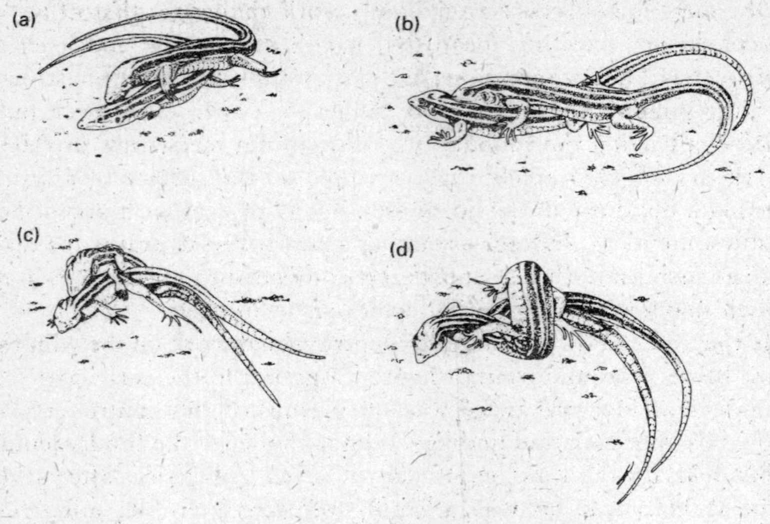

Figure 6.1. Sexual behaviour in C. *uniparens* (redrawn by Steven W. Allison from Myers, 1990, p. 273).

sexuality that cannot be separated and analysed in normal sexual species, where the complicating factor of male heredity is always present.

As soon as Crews started work on *Cnemidophorus* he noticed what at first sight was a bizarre pattern of behaviour. These non-sexual lizards, who did not need to mate, sometimes mounted each other, behaving just like other sexual lizards. It was this observation which previous researchers had ignored, or chosen to ignore, which lies at the heart of the controversy.

The behaviour of significance to our story is reproduced in the series of illustrations shown in figure 6.1. The sequence appears to be simple enough. One active female climbs onto the back of another passive female, curves its tail around its partner's body so that their sexual organs come into contact, strokes the neck and back, and rides on top of the other for one to five minutes. All biologists agree that this is what happens. They disagree over the meaning to be given to the observations.

For Crews and his co-worker Fitzgerald, the lizard's strange behaviour (repeatedly observed with different lizards) was clearly sexually related. Indeed, they thought that what they had seen was so significant that they presented it as a new and important scientific discovery about parthenogenetic species. The courtship routine followed by the copulatory behaviour seemed remarkably similar to ordinary mating which Crews had observed in other closely related sexual species. Furthermore, dissection and palpation (examining by touch), of the lizards revealed its sexual significance. The courted animal appeared to be reproductively active, 'having ovaries containing large, preovulatory follicles, while the courting animal was either reproductively inactive or postovulatory, having ovaries containing only small undeveloped follicles'. This difference raised general questions about the function of the pseudo-copulatory behaviour for sexuality, such as its possible role in priming reproductive mechanisms.

If Crews thought he had made a major discovery, other biologists were not so sure. Some were outright sceptics. Two of the best-known researchers into this genus of lizard, Orlando Cuellar of the University of Utah, who in the early 1970s had shown the chromosomal mechanisms of parthenogenesis, and C. J. Cole of the American Museum of Natural History, who pioneered the physiological study of the genus, soon disputed Crews' claims. For these scientists, who had spent years studying *Cnemidophorus* and in particular learning how to maintain them in captivity, Crews was an inexperienced upstart. Rather than carefully observing the lizards over lengthy periods, he had, in their view, immediately seized upon a peculiar piece of behaviour, noticed in a very few animals, and blown it up into a sensational claim. Cuellar and Cole may have been particularly irked that *Time* magazine had picked up on the story; the sexual exploits of lizards made for compelling media coverage.

The first response of Cuellar and Cole was to attempt to play down the aberrant behaviour. They claimed that there was nothing particularly novel or surprising going on, since others (including themselves) had observed such activity among lizards before. Also Crews was simply wrong in claiming any general significance for the study of parthenogenetic species. The behaviour he had observed was trivial: it was unnatural and a product of captivity. Moreover a more experienced worker would not have been led astray and would have chosen to ignore it for the artefact it undoubtedly was. The key issue, then, was whether the lizard's behaviour was an artefact, produced by the overcrowded conditions of captivity, as the critics asserted, or an essential and previously neglected part of reproductive behaviour.

One feature of scientific controversies is that they bring into sharp focus the competence of the protagonists. Normally in science ability is taken for granted. However, in a controversy the specific scientific issues at stake and the abilities of the scientists involved are difficult to disentangle. In the ensuing debate between Crews and his critics the need for all the researchers to establish their skill became paramount.

Much of the controversy has taken place in the published scientific literature and one indication of the increasing importance attached to the establishment of competence is the expansion of the normally brief 'methods' sections of the papers. In Crews and Fitzgerald's original paper the method section was simply a few lines which accompanied photographs of the lizards. However, by the time it comes to rebutting their critics five years later, there is a remarkable amount of detail concerning the regimen of care of the lizards, the observational procedures followed and so on. As the controversy develops, the skills and competence necessary to make these sorts of observation also become an issue. For instance, in his published attack on Crews, Orlando Cuellar refers to his own long experience (over a decade) observing captive *Cnemidophorus* produce eggs, and his 'precise knowledge' of the reproductive cycle. He states that, although he has seen behaviour such as that observed by Crews sporadically on and off for fifteen years in the laboratory, it is insignificant.

In the same way, Cole and Townsend, in a rebuttal of Crews and Fitzgerald, emphasise their own skills as observers, stressing the detail and duration of their observations (in contrast to the short period of Crews and Fitzgerald's work), and the fine-grained nature of their behaviour categorisation system. They even mention where the lizards were kept (in their offices), and that they cared for the animals personally. Again such details never normally appear in routine research reports.

Such personal appeals to a scientist's own skills and reconstructions of the details of everyday work in the lab produce, however, an unintended effect. They make science look more like other areas of activity which are carried out in the mundane world of offices and which depend on skill.

It is no accident that the routine scientific paper plays down such factors. It is the absence of these discussions which makes science look like a special activity; scientists become merely mediators or passive observers of Nature. Because the establishment of skill and competence becomes important during a controversy we start to see better what goes into the making of science. Processes which are normally hidden become visible.

Ironically when Crews and his colleagues responded to Cuellar they made his appeal to his own diligence and experience count against him. They took his admission that he had indeed seen the pseudo-copulatory behaviour as a confirmation of their own observations. They then went on to treat his failure to realise its significance as stemming from his own preconceptions. This is part of a general strategy which Crews has used against his critics whereby he portrays them as being stick-in-the-mud, paradigm bound, and caught up in the old traditions, rather than seeing what is there to be seen. This 'young Turks' strategy is not unfamiliar in scientific controversy.

Part of the argument concerning competence centres on the carefulness of the observers. In this case the critics claim that Crews and Fitzgerald simply have not been careful enough in their observations. The argument about carefulness, however, like most arguments in a controversy, can cut both ways. This line is taken by Crews and his group in their response to Cole and Townsend; they pick upon an apparent lack of rigour in the methods followed. They note that Cole and Townsend assess the reproductive state of the lizards from a visual inspection of abdominal distension. This, they claim, is inadequate as it is well known that palpation is also needed. In an ingenious move, they actually cite Crews' other critic, Cuellar, in support of this requirement.

Accusations of carelessness are ineffective in resolving disputes because they tend to circularity. Everyone knows that the careful scientist will find the 'truth', while the careless observer gets it wrong. But what there is to find is exactly the point at issue. If you believe pseudo-copulation is a genuine phenomenon then Crews appears to have been careful and his critics careless; conversely if pseudo-copulation is taken to be an artefact then it is his critics who have been careful and Crews careless. Care, in and of itself, like most such factors in a controversy, cannot provide an independent means to settle the issue. We are back in the experimenter's regress with a vengeance.

If general attributions of skill and competence cannot settle the controversy, what about matters of fact? As we have argued above, matters of fact are inseparable from the skills of the scientist used to produce them. Thus when the critics make a specific claim in an attempt to refute Crews, it is no surprise to find again that issues of competence are never far from the surface. The claim made by Cuellar, and Cole and Townsend, that the copulatory-like behaviour of the lizards stems from overcrowded conditions lies at the core of the controversy. It is answered by Crews in the following way. In his later articles, as mentioned above, he goes into great detail concerning his methods. The exact conditions under which his lizards are kept are given. Having done this, he is able to turn the tables on his critics by claiming that they present no specific data themselves to show that crowded conditions will lead to the artefactual copulation. 'They do not give the dimensions of the cages used, nor the number of animals housed per cage' (quoted in Myers, 1990, p. 125). With this move, it is Crews who appears to have been painstakingly careful in the very area where his critics have chosen to make their attack; the critics, on the other hand, are made to look cavalier in their accusation.

One way in which this controversy in biology appears to differ from the controversies in physics examined in this book is that very few new data are generated during the course of the controversy. The grounds of the debate seem to be constantly switching in the process of trying to find the right interpretation for previous observations. In physics, experiments serve as a way of focussing the debate. In this area of biology, experiments are seldom possible. Rather, attention is constantly drawn to evidence that is missing from the rival side's position – such as the evidence on crowded conditions leading to pseudo-copulation as mentioned by Crews in response to Cole and Townsend.

The most salient piece of negative evidence in the whole debate is simply that no-one, including Crews and Fitzgerald, has ever seen pseudo-copulation of lizards in the field. Cole and Townsend make much of this point, mentioning that the most thorough study of *Cnemidophorus* in the wild does not include it. As might be expected, Crews' and his group's response is up to the job. Again they turn the tables on the critics. They point out that such behaviour might well occur, but are observations in the wild capable of documenting it? It is well known that *Cnemidophorus* is a very shy species and that even matings in the ordinary sexual lizard are observed infrequently. So where better to observe such delicate phenomena than in captivity!

Love bites and hand waving

Often in the course of a scientific controversy previously ignored minutiae become highly relevant and hotly debated. As both sides try to cast doubt upon the others' arguments, more and more additional pieces of evidence get brought in. In the present case the number of 'love bites' the lizards underwent and whether or not they wave their hands as a sign of sexual submission both became important.

Cuellar argued that in species he had collected in the wild he had rarely seen any 'copulation bites' and more would be expected if pseudo-copulation was routine. The answer Crews and his group gave was again to reverse the argument by pointing out that if Cuellar was right then it would mean that normal sexual lizards were not mating either! The answer, they suggested, was that such bites are not a natural inscription of mating. To try to substantiate their point they examined the corpses of 1000 dead female lizards from a sexual species and found only 3% had marks on their backs and sides and, further, that the same frequency of males possessed such marks. So in this way Crews managed to turn the evidence produced by Cuellar back against him. Marks are most certainly found on dead lizards, but as they are found on males as well they are probably produced by aggressive behaviour.

Hand waving became significant in a postscript added by Cole and Townsend to their rebuttal of Crews. They criticise Crews for 'erroneously' relying on the lizards' lifting of the hand as an indication of submissiveness. Instead, according to them, it is merely a sign that the lizard is basking. Again it is the competence of the researchers which is under attack. A researcher who cannot tell basking from hand waving has a credibility problem. Although Crews does not seem to have responded in public to this particular criticism, from what has gone above the reader can speculate about the possible lines of argument Crews could have adopted in defence.

An honorable draw

So where does this controversy stand today? The current consensus is that Crews and his critics have battled to an honorable draw. Both sides have given their version of the endocrinology of *Cnemidophorus* in separate articles in the *Scientific American* and both continue to work within their rather different approaches.

The even-handed view which we have presented as we have followed the twists and turns of the debate is not likely to be shared by the protagonists. Their own arguments and positions are, of course, compelling, indeed irresistible to them. In presenting a neutral account we risk disappointing both sides.

Many scientists are wary of getting entangled in controversies and perceive them to be the repository of shoddy science. This can mean that denying you are party to a controversy can itself be a tactic in such disputes. We see it happening in the lizard controversy. In writing their articles in *Scientific American* both sides avoided any explicit reference to the controversy at all.

One way to close down a controversy is to rewrite history such that the dispute seems premature: an over-reaction of an under-developed field. Crews, in particular, in his later writing has presented his first paper and the reaction to it as having this character. For Crews it was an unfortunate debate which was characterised by a lack of firm experimental tests and decisive evidence. By appealing to the rhetoric of experiment and testing, something to which his methodology of working with lizards in captivity is ideally suited, Crews can appear to have found a way to have advanced beyond the earlier controversy. Whether this rhetoric succeeds remains to be seen.

One question has been left unanswered. Do *Cnemidophorus*

lizards indeed exhibit pseudo-copulatory behaviour which is relevant to their reproduction? Despite five years of research and debate the answer appears to be that we do not know. According to one group of respected scientists they do; according to another group they do not. As always the facts of nature are settled within the field of human argument.

7

Set the controls for the heart of the sun: the strange story of the missing solar neutrinos

The many stars we see burning in the night sky have one thing in common. They all convert matter into energy by a process known as nuclear fusion. This is the same process that occurs in hydrogen bombs. Because stars are continually eating up their own mass of hydrogen over time, they slowly change. The process of change or evolution is usually gradual, but can have dramatic moments such as the cataclysmic end of a star in a huge explosion, a supernova. The changing history of stars, including our own sun, is described by stellar evolution theory: one of the most fundamental theories in modern astrophysics. This theory successfully explains the different transitions undergone by most stars. For astronomers and astrophysicists, stellar evolution theory is taken for granted as much as Darwin's theory of evolution is for biologists.

Yet, despite the undoubted successes of the theory, its central assumption – that nuclear fusion is the source of a star's energy – has only recently been directly tested.

In 1967, Ray Davis, of the Brookhaven National Laboratory tried to detect solar neutrinos: sub-nuclear particles produced by nuclear fusion in our own sun. This was the first direct experimental test of stellar evolution theory. All other radiation coming from the sun is the result of processes that took place millions of years earlier. For example, light rays take millions of years to escape from the sun's core as they work their way to the surface. Neutrinos, because they interact so little with matter, travel straight out of the sun. Their detection on the earth would tell us what was happening in the core of the sun only 8 minutes earlier (the time the neutrinos take to travel from the sun to the earth). Solar neutrinos thus provide a direct test of whether our nearest star, the sun, has fusion as its energy source.

Precisely because neutrinos interact so little with matter, they are very very hard to detect. On average a neutrino can travel through a million million miles of lead before it is stopped. Detecting neutrinos was always going to be a difficult project! Davis' experiment is rather unusual. He used a vast tank of chlorine-rich cleaning fluid, the size of an Olympic swimming pool, buried deep underground in a disused mine shaft. Every month Davis dredges this tank searching for a radioactive form of argon, produced by the reaction of incoming neutrinos with chlorine. Unfortunately particles from outer space, known as cosmic rays, also trigger the reaction and this is why the experiment must be located deep underground to provide enough shielding to absorb the unwanted rays. The radioactive argon, once extracted from the tank, is placed in a very sensitive radioactive detector (a form of geiger counter), where the exact amount formed can be measured.

This experiment, which must be one of the most peculiar of modern science, has had a baffling outcome. The predicted neutrino fluxes are not there. A test which was intended as the crowning glory of stellar evolution theory has instead produced consternation. It is scarcely imaginable that stars do not have nuclear fusion as their energy source, so what has gone wrong? The experiment has been checked and rechecked, theories have been juggled, and models and assumptions have been carefully probed for errors. Thus far, however, no-one is sure what has gone wrong. Even today, with second-generation experiments 'coming on the air' (or more accurately 'going underground' since all such experiments need shielding from cosmic rays), it is by no means clear what the outcome will be.

This then is a classic case of a confrontation between experiment and theory. The theoretical realm and the experimental realm cannot, however, be so easily separated. In the solar-neutrino case, theorists and experimentalists have been collaborating for years to reach a conclusion.

In the first part of our story we will examine how the scientists built the partnership from which the experiment was born. The reception of the results of Davis' experiment, which we deal with in the second part, can only be understood against this background.

Just as the solar-neutrino experiment is supposed to give us a glimpse into the heart of the sun, the solar-neutrino *episode* gives us a glimpse of what happens in the heart of science when things do not turn out as expected. Strangely, we shall encounter science become 'unmade'.

Although the theoretical models used to calculate the solar-neutrino flux are complex (they are run on large computers), and the experiment is mind-boggling in its sensitivity (a handful of argon atoms are searched for in a tank containing billions upon billions of atoms), when the experiment was first thought of, the procedures were considered routine. Ray Davis, who is a chemist, perhaps over-modestly describes his experiment as merely a matter of 'plumbing'. Indeed, in the early 1960s, so confident was the physics community that Davis would confirm stellar evolution theory that a whole series of underground 'telescopes' were planned to detect neutrinos from a range of different cosmic sources. Such plans were shelved after Davis' first results became known. What were formerly taken to be well-understood areas of science became problematic and contentious. The robust became fragile, the closed open, and the certain uncertain. The intricate network of ties between theory and experiment was threatened with rupture. That the rupture has thus far been contained; that the experimental results have stood the test of time; and that the structure of stellar evolution theory remains in place, is a puzzle. We are *not* witnessing the collapse characteristic of a scientific revolution, yet, on the other hand, it is not quite 'business as usual'.

PART 1. BUILDING EXPERIMENTS AND PARTNERSHIPS

Experiments, like any outcome of human activity, do not arrive *de novo*. When Ray Davis 'switched on' his apparatus in the summer of 1967 to look for the expected flux of neutrinos, the previous 20 years of hard work by himself and others was at stake. Of particular importance was a unique partnership between Davis and a group of nuclear astrophysicists (nuclear astrophysics is nuclear physics applied to astronomy), at the Kellogg Radiation Laboratory of the California Institute of Technology, headed by William Fowler.

The neutrino has always held a special fascination for experimenters because it is one of the most elusive and therefore challenging particles to detect. First postulated by Wolfgang Pauli in 1930 as a purely theoretical entity needed to make theories of radioactive decay consistent, the neutrino was thought to have zero mass and zero electric charge. A kind of reverse radioactivity reaction was one of the few ways to detect this elusive particle. In such reactions a neutrino is absorbed by the nucleus of an atom to form a new element which is unstable and in turn decays. Separating out the few atoms of the newly formed element from the billions upon billions of target atoms is a technically daunting task. Carrying out this task is what Davis, who had long been interested in neutrino detection, set out to do.

The experimental technique Davis used came from the hybrid field of radioactivity and chemistry, known as radio-chemistry. The idea was to use chemistry to separate out the newly formed radioactive element (argon) from the target material. Davis achieved this by having the target in liquid form and purging it with helium gas, thus sweeping out the accumulated argon atoms. The exact quantity of argon formed could then be measured by counting its characteristic decays. In order to help separate argon decays from the background radiation Davis shielded his counter in a First-World-War gun barrel made of steel with low natural radioactivity.

The use of the chlorine–argon reaction for neutrino detection was first suggested by physicists Bruno Pontecorvo and Louis Alvarez. Alvarez's involvement was particularly important. As was the case for so much post-war physics, the idea stemmed from war-time work. Alvarez had devised a new method to determine whether the Germans were building an atomic bomb. This was a mobile radiochemical detector which could be placed in a bomber and could be used to search for radioactive emissions from smoke-stacks when flown over Germany (none were found).

Davis took over Alvarez's ideas and by 1955 he had built a small working detector using 550 gallons of cleaning fluid. Of course, he could not detect anything unless he had a source of neutrinos. One of the most likely sources was thought to be nuclear power plants and thus Davis installed his detector at the Savannah River nuclear power reactor. At the same time and place Frederick Reines and Clyde Cowan were making their now historic measurements which provided the first detection of the free neutrino. Unfortunately for Davis it turned out that his apparatus was not sensitive to the types of neutrino produced in nuclear reactors. Davis now faced a dilemma. He had developed a promising detection system, but he had no neutrinos to detect. It was William Fowler who provided the way out of the dilemma.

Collaboration with Cal Tech

At Cal Tech, William Fowler was watching Davis's work closely. Nuclear astrophysics as a discipline had taken off in the 1930s following on from Eddington and Jean's pioneering achievement in identifying nuclear reactions as the most likely source of the sun's energy (this is the same Eddington as encountered in chapter 2). By the end of the 1950s, after many laboratory measurements of nuclear reactions, the detailed cycles of nuclear reactions in our own sun had been determined. In 1957 a comprehensive theory of how lighter elements are synthesised into heavier elements in stars was outlined by Fowler and his co-workers at Cal Tech. This was one of the highpoints of the discipline – it appeared to explain how all familiar substances were formed from the lightest element of all, hydrogen.

In 1958 one of the reaction rates crucial to the nuclear reaction cycle in the sun was remeasured and found to have been in error. It looked as if the sun produced some fairly high-energy neutrinos, which Davis should be able to detect. Fowler immediately alerted Davis to the possibility and from then on the two collaborated in order to bring the detector plans to fruition. At the time Fowler considered the detection of solar neutrinos to be the 'icing on the cake' of stellar evolution theory.

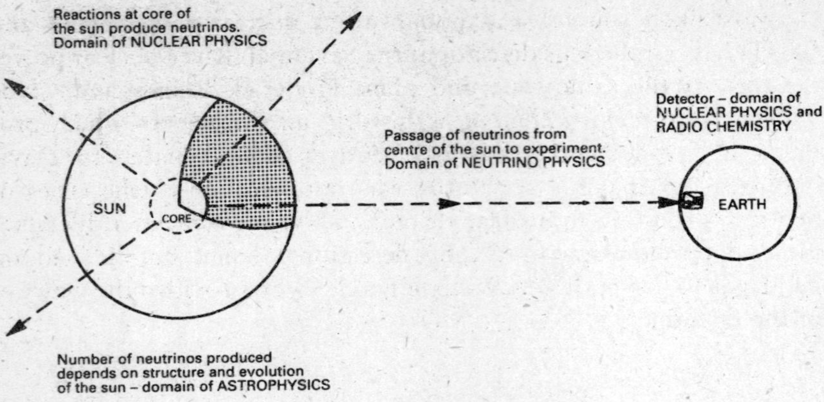

Figure 7.1: The different domains of solar-neutrino science.

Bahcall: a house theorist away from home

The Cal Tech end of the partnership with Davis centred upon a young post-doctoral student of Fowler's, John Bahcall. If solar neutrinos were to be Fowler's icing on the cake, they proved to be John Bahcall's bread and butter. Solar neutrinos became a dominant theme of Bahcall's subsequent career. By the time Davis was ready to make measurements it was Bahcall's career as much as Davis' that was at stake. The need for scientists to act in a concerted manner over a period of time as they pursue their careers is well illustrated by Bahcall's involvement.

Bahcall was a theoretical physicist and, as well as providing theoretical expertise, his job was to coordinate the Cal Tech effort. The prediction of the number of neutrinos Davis should expect to measure was a complex task requiring a variety of different sorts of knowledge. When Bahcall did not have the requisite expertise himself, he proved very adept (with Fowler's support) at recruiting others to help him.

The detailed prediction involved nuclear physics, astrophysics, neutrino physics, as well as radio-chemistry. The different domains of solar-neutrino physics are shown in figure 7.1.

Nuclear physics was needed both to measure the nuclear reaction rates in the sun and to calculate the interaction between neutrinos and chlorine in the detector. Since all the relevant nuclear reaction rates are measured in the laboratory at much higher energies than occur in the core of the sun, extrapolations to lower energies have to be made. These measurements and consequent estimates are often uncertain, and throughout the history of the solar-neutrino problem reaction rates have been revised as different measurements and calculations have been made. The Kellogg Radiation Laboratory housed some of the leading nuclear physicists. Bahcall soon enlisted their help in remeasuring many of the crucial nuclear parameters.

Another key element in calculating the neutrino fluxes is astrophysics. This is required to produce a detailed model of the sun's structure and evolution. The solar evolution is modelled on a computer over the equivalent of the 4.5 billion years life of the sun. Many data about the sun, such as the composition of its constituent elements, have to be fed into the model. Such input data were constantly revised. The solar model was constructed by specialists at Cal Tech. The largest component of the neutrino flux which Davis was expected to detect came from one sub-branch of the main hydrogen fusion chain of nuclear reactions in the sun. These high-energy neutrinos turned out to be extraordinarily temperature sensitive and critically dependent on the details of the solar-model. Expertise in neutrino physics was also required in order to determine what happened to the neutrinos in their passage through the sun and on their long journey to the earth.

As well as working on the prediction of the neutrino fluxes, Bahcall helped Davis with theoretical problems that arose in connection with the design of the experiment, such as, for instance, what the likely cosmic ray background might be, when best to take samples from the tank, and so on. In his own words he became the 'house theorist'. He eventually became a consultant to the Brookhaven National Laboratory where Davis worked and thus was paid for his services by the same 'house'.

Funding the experiment

Davis estimated the cost of the experiment to be approximately \$600 000. In the 1960s this was a large sum to obtain for one experiment which, unlike particle accelerators, could be used to produce only one sort of measurement. Fowler was extremely influential in the process of obtaining the funding. He constantly advised Davis and Bahcall and elicited support from his own colleagues. Soundings were taken with all likely sources of support: the Atomic Energy Commission, the National Science Foundation and NASA.

It is naive to think that scientists obtain funding merely by writing a compelling grant proposal. To get funding for a major facility scientists have to engage in political lobbying and other forms of persuasion. In raising the money for Davis' experiment the following were important: the publication by Davis and Bahcall of their results and plans in the leading physics journal, *Physical Review Letters*; the use of the highly influential Kellogg Radiation Laboratory 'Orange and Lemon Aid' Preprint series in circulating information to the scientific community about what was happening; and coverage in the scientific and popular press – articles about solar neutrinos appeared in both *Time* and *Newsweek*. Of most importance was a letter to the Atomic Energy Commission which Fowler wrote at the bidding of Davis' departmental chairman, Richard Dodson. In this letter Fowler strongly urged that the experiment be funded. Dodson and Fowler were old friends and former colleagues at Cal Tech. It seems that at the time the Atomic Energy Commission did not use formal peer review, and Fowler's 'fine letter' (Dodson's words) provided the needed technical acclaim to ensure funding.

Of course, all these efforts to raise funding turned on the scientific merits of the case. The experiment was widely billed as a 'crucial' direct test of stellar evolution theory. Two things about the rhetoric used at the time are worth noting. Firstly, although undoubtedly more direct than other ways of measuring radiation from the sun's core, the neutrinos Davis expected to detect came from one highly temperature-sensitive sub-branch of the chain of hydrogen reactions. A more direct test would be of the fundamental hydrogen fusion reaction itself. The second-generation experiments now starting to produce results are sensitive to neutrinos from this reaction. Yet, in the effort to obtain funding, these new experiments too have been billed as 'crucial'. The rhetoric of 'cruciality' is clearly context dependent. There can be little doubt that when seeking hard-pressed dispensers of funds for large sums of money it helps to be doing something crucial.

The second thing to note is that many of the scientists whose support was needed for the experiment were nuclear and particle physicists. Such physicists, brought up on 'hard-nosed' laboratory science, were sceptical of astrophysics which they regarded as being much less precise. Many physicists were cautious about funding an experiment based upon astrophysics. One such sceptic was nuclear physicist Maurice Goldhaber, the Director of the Brookhaven National Laboratory. His support was crucial. Bahcall paid a special visit to Brookhaven to add his voice to the effort to persuade Goldhaber that the predictions were reliable and the experiment feasible.

In order to convince sceptics such as Goldhaber it was in Bahcall's interests to have a clear-cut prediction of a large signal which Davis could detect without ambiguity. There is some evidence that the predictions of the flux of solar neutrinos varied with physicists' need for funding. Figure 7.2 shows the predicted solar neutrino flux in SNUs (solar neutrino units) over time. It reveals that at the moment when the experiment was funded in 1964 the predicted flux was high (40 SNU). It can also be seen that immediately afterwards the predicted flux started to come down, and that by the time Davis got his first results in 1967 it had fallen to a much lower figure (19 SNU). Happily Davis managed to obtain greater sensitivity by improvements in the detection process, but several scientists commented that the experiment would never have been funded if the smaller levels of fluxes predicted in 1967 had been predicted earlier, in 1964 when the experiment was funded.

Many of the changes in the predicted flux came from parameters beyond Bahcall's immediate control, such as remeasurements of nuclear reaction rates and changes in other parameters. However, the timing of the push for funding, and the realisation (only after funding had been awarded) that one of the most important nuclear reaction rates had been incorrectly extrapolated to low energies, tended to work in favour of an overly optimistic prediction in 1964. The interdependence of theory and experiment could scarcely be clearer.

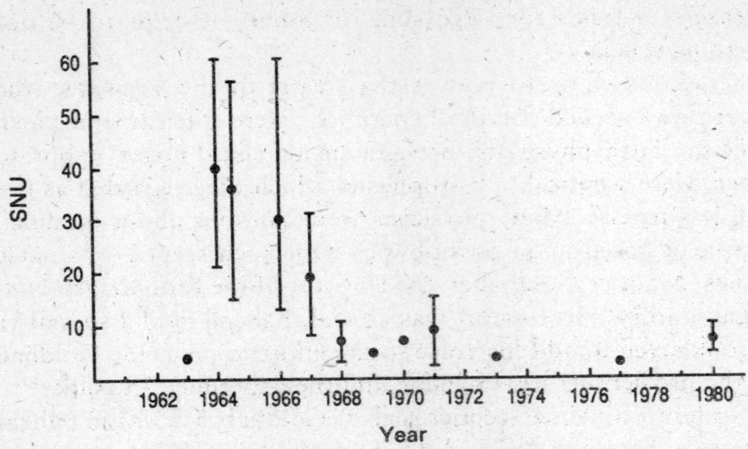

Figure 7.2. Solar neutrino flux (redrawn by Steven W. Allison from Pinch, 1986, p. 39).

Building the experiment

If Bahcall was engaged in unconventional activities for a theoretical physicist, Davis too faced some unusual tasks. Having obtained the necessary funding, he needed to find a deep mine shaft in which to locate his experiment. This proved to be far from easy, not only because of physical constraints such as the depth and stability of rock, but also because most mine owners could see little merit in housing an inconvenient and possibly dangerous experiment in their mines. Davis spent much of 1964 in negotiation with mine owners. Finally the Homestake Mining Company agreed to go ahead with the project once they realised that it was sponsored by the Atomic Energy Commission. It was no accident that the Atomic Energy Commission were consumers of the product of another important Homestake mining venture: uranium.

The building of the experiment involved Davis in extensive liaisons with the mining company and other commercial companies who helped fabricate the tank and associated equipment and deliver the cleaning fluid to the mine. (The cleaning fluid is actually on loan and may one day be returned for its more usual purpose!) In the end the local miners became enthusiastic about the experiment and several issues of the Homestake newspaper were devoted to the story.

It is a very impoverished view of science which treats theorists simply as producers of new ideas, and experimenters as the people who test or verify such ideas. As we have seen, doing theory and experiment are far more interesting than that. Theory and experiment are not independent activities. They are linked through and through, and form part of a wider network of ties between scientists. If it had not been for the collaboration of theoreticians and experimenters, and in particular the influence of the powerful group of Cal Tech scientists under William Fowler's leadership, the solar-neutrino experiment would never have happened.

PART 2. SCIENCE UNMADE

We will now turn to examine what happened when, against all expectations, Davis reported his negative result. Unlike some of the other cases discussed in this volume which involve a clash between theory and experiment, Davis' experiment has not lost credibility. For a while severe doubts were raised about his experimental method – perhaps somewhere in the vast tank of cleaning fluid he was losing a few atoms of argon. Davis, however, was able to survive such criticism and indeed eventually emerge with an enhanced reputation as a careful experimenter. The theorists too, and Bahcall in particular, have by-and-large managed to live with the result, although, as we shall see, Bahcall for a time felt that any contradiction between theory and experiment was not compelling.

The main feature of the period, once it was widely recognised that the solar-neutrino problem did indeed exist, has been a process of questioning and examination; just about every assumption upon which the scientific basis of the project was based has come under challenge. It is in such challenges that we can catch a glimpse of science as it becomes 'unmade'.

The first results

Davis' first results were obtained in August 1967. They indicated a very low signal, that is, a very low flux of neutrinos. Indeed the signal was so low that it could not be reported as a number (of neutrinos detected) with a possible error, but only as the upper limit: 6 SNU. In other words the signal was no greater than 6 SNU and this signal might result from background radiation alone. Improvements in the detection technique meant that by early 1968 Davis could set an even lower limit on the neutrino fluxes of 3 SNU. Davis, who had been working with this detection technique for most of his career, did not doubt that his result was correct. In view of its importance, however, he invited two fellow Brookhaven chemists to check his work. They could find nothing wrong. As an added precaution Davis calibrated his experiment by irradiating his tank with a neutron source which also produced the same isotope of argon as he detected. He recovered the expected number of argon atoms which seemed again to indicate that all was working well. However, this test was not taken to be compelling by everyone, as we shall see below. By this stage (May 1968) Davis felt confident enough to publish his result. In preliminary reports of his findings he stressed that his result was five times below the predicted signal of 19 SNU.

Bahcall's reaction

Davis' confidence that his result was out of line with theory was not shared by Bahcall. As soon as Bahcall learnt of Davis' low result (he was, of course, in continual contact), he went to work with yet more 'fine-tuning' of the theoretical 'prediction'. New measurements of various parameters were included which reduced the prediction to 7.5 SNU (with an error bar of 3 SNU). This enabled Bahcall to report by May 1968 that the 'present results of Davis . . . are not in obvious conflict with the theory of stellar structure'.

At this point Bahcall very much wanted Davis' experiment to be in agreement with his 'prediction'. With Davis reporting ever lower results, Bahcall became more and more depressed. Most of the other theorists shared Bahcall's concerns and were hoping against hope that the conflict would go away. A lot had been invested in this experiment. There was even talk of a Nobel Prize in the offing if only Davis' experiment would 'come out right'.

Iben's reaction

That a contradiction between theory and experiment existed was first and most forcefully recognised not by Bahcall, but by an old colleague of his from Cal Tech days, Icko Iben. Iben was a solar model specialist who had been part of the Cal Tech team which made the 1964 prediction. Iben now took a rather jaundiced view of what Bahcall was doing. For him, Bahcall was being disingenuous, abandoning the previously bold predictions of a high flux and using rather arbitrary values for parameters in order to try and lower the flux. In Iben's mind there was little doubt that there was a conflict and he used his own solar models to demonstrate its extent. A potentially acrimonious dispute between the two theorists was avoided, however, when shortly afterwards (in 1969) Bahcall, too, went on record proclaiming there to be a discrepancy. The solar-neutrino problem was now officially born.

The disagreement between Bahcall and Iben reminds us once more how flexible the 'prediction' with its many inputs could be. This episode also shows that judging the outcome of a test of a theory is not always straightforward. It is not simply a matter of inspecting theoretical prediction and experimental result as some philosophers believe. Interpretation is always involved. Bahcall and Iben were both highly competent theorists who were well-acquainted with the relevant scientific issues, yet in 1967 they drew rather different conclusions.

Bahcall now became one of the leading advocates of the view that there was a discrepancy – so much so that he has even fought battles with other scientists who were less enthusiastic about the extent and importance of the solar-neutrino problem. Although it is hazardous imputing strategies to individual scientists, and we should be wary of any simple-minded models of scientists as rational calculators who always try to promote what is in their best career interests, we can nevertheless speculate as to what rationale Bahcall might have had for his dramatic change in position.

His initial resistance to the idea that there was a conflict can be understood as a response to his previous involvement with the experiment. In 1967 Bahcall rightly or wrongly believed that further progress in his career depended upon Davis getting the right answer. However, the longer he held to the view that there was no conflict, while other theorists such as Iben who had less at stake in the project drew opposite conclusions, the more tenuous his position became. An indication of the kind of pressure he was under at the time comes from a conversation which Bahcall recalls having had with the famous Cal Tech physicist, Richard Feynman. Feynman apparently advised the young Bahcall that he had done nothing wrong and that if there was a contradiction this made the result *more* rather than less important. It seems Bahcall took Feynman's advice to heart. Furthermore, it seems to have been good advice. Bahcall has managed to continue to make a career out of solar neutrinos by stressing the scientific importance of the problem. His career does not seem to have suffered either; he has won prizes for his work on solar neutrinos and currently holds the highly prestigious post of Professor of Astronomy and Astrophysics at the Princeton Institute for Advanced Study.

Ray Davis: an ideal experimenter

With the conflict between theory and experiment now publicly recognised by the theorists, the heat was back on Davis to make sure that the problem did not reside with him. In most controversies of this type, as we have seen elsewhere in this volume, other scientists become involved in attempts to repeat the original experiment; in this case the experiment was too daunting and costly. This placed a special onus on Davis. Although he felt further tests of his procedures were largely a waste of time in terms of learning any new science, he saw the need to convince the more sceptical community of astrophysicists.

Throughout, Davis has made a point of following up and carrying out their suggestions, no matter how out-landish they might appear.

The strategy seems to have paid off because over the years Davis has acquired something of a reputation as the ideal experimenter. Indeed at one meeting in 1978 he was heralded as an unsung 'scientific hero' and he is widely regarded as one of the best experimenters in modern science. The ideal experimenter's profile which Davis cultivated is that of openness, caution, and modesty. There can be little doubt that acquiring such a profile helps an experimenter to maintain credibility. That Davis had already built a partnership with the theoreticians can now be seen to go some way towards explaining why his result has been taken so seriously. Having invested so much in him and his experiment, and having worked with him over the years, the theoreticians could not easily abandon him.

Among the new tests Davis agreed to perform was the introduction of 500 atoms of argon directly into his tank. Davis went on to recover the argon with the expected efficiency. He also persuaded some Brookhaven chemists to look for an anomalous form of argon which might remain trapped in the tank. They could find none. However, to repeat a familiar theme from other parts of this book, no experiment is alone definitive, and loop-holes can always be found by a determined critic. In 1976 such a determined critic appeared in the shape of a sceptical astrophysicist, Kenneth Jacobs.

Argon trapping

Jacobs was worried that Davis' experiment had never been repeated and he drew analogies with other experiments, such as Weber's gravity wave detector (discussed in chapter 5), where a signal near the noise was used as a basis to challenge established theories, and where in the long run the experiment had become discredited. Jacobs maintained that it was most likely that argon was being trapped somewhere, thus explaining the low result. He proposed a possible mechanism for such trapping in the form of weak 'polymerisation' which liquid hydro-carbons similar to Davis' cleaning fluid were known to undergo. He remained unconvinced that all the previous tests ruled out this possibility.

Jacobs' doubts could always be raised because of the logic of the types of calibration experiment Davis was forced to undertake.

Calibration tests by their very nature always involve differences when compared with what happens in an actual experimental run. For example, the calibration Davis used relied on ready-made argon atoms rather than atoms formed by neutrino interaction. Even when argon atoms were deliberately formed by fast neutron bombardment the chains of reaction were quite different from those involved in the case of neutrinos from the sun. Differences between a calibration and an experiment itself always exist. A compelling calibration is one where the importance of such differences seems small so that calibration is as much like the 'real thing' as possible, but 'seeming small' is a variable phenomenon.

Differences between experiments, as we see in other chapters of this book, always give grounds for doubt. Whether or not such doubts are raised depends on how far a scientist is prepared to challenge the conventional wisdom which holds such differences to be insignificant. Jacobs, as we have seen, was prepared to challenge that wisdom and for him the differences revealed a chink through which his argon-trapping hypothesis could sneak.

There was a complex test which was widely regarded as ruling out trapping. Davis eventually performed this test successfully. We do not know if Jacobs could have questioned this as well, because he failed to get tenure at his university and quit science altogether. Although the matter has rested here, if someone else as determined as Jacobs were to appear on the scene . . .

Solutions to the problem

Radio-chemistry aside, the overwhelming response to Davis' results has been to question one or more of the complicated chain of assumptions in the nuclear physics, astrophysics or neutrino physics which form the basis of the predicted neutrino fluxes. By 1978 over 400 papers had been published proposing 'solutions' to the solar-neutrino problem. Perhaps unsurprisingly it is in the area of astrophysics that most solutions have been canvassed. We have already remarked on the extraordinary temperature sensitivity of the neutrinos Davis sought to detect and many solutions have involved modifications to the solar model which lower the sun's central temperature. For instance, mixing of cooler material from the exterior of the sun into the hot core (like a giant cauldron) would reduce the neutrino fluxes. A reduction would also be obtained if the sun had become contaminated by heavy elements early on in its history, perhaps as a result of a collision with another celestial body. In the area of nuclear physics it has been suggested that the extrapolations of reaction rates to low energies are not sound. One of the strongest candidate solutions is that of 'neutrino oscillation'. Over the years Davis' result has consistently been about one third less than the best theoretical prediction. Since there are three types of neutrino and Davis' experiment is only sensitive to one sort, the proposal is that the neutrinos are produced in one state in the sun but oscillate between their three states in the long journey to the earth, and Davis only picks up a third of his expected signal.

Some of the proposed solutions have been almost bizarre: the sun is not burning hydrogen at all; or a fundamental theory, such as weak interaction theory, which governs the interaction between neutrinos and chlorine, is in error. Many solutions have not been rebutted and remain unremarked upon in the literature. Others have been given careful consideration and rejected on a variety of grounds. Often such solutions have proved difficult to rule out altogether and scientists have had to resort to notions such as that they are *ad hoc*, or 'aesthetically unappealing'. Overall none of the solutions has yet gained universal assent. On the other hand, stellar evolution theory has not been overthrown. The solar-neutrino result has been treated as an anomaly; something to be put aside for the time being.

An experiment into the nature of science

Although no challenge has yet gained consensus as *the solution* to the solar-neutrino problem, such challenges are interesting because they reveal a world of doubt and uncertainty which lies behind even the most well-established areas of knowledge. Before 1967, the project to detect solar neutrinos seemed to rest upon a solid structure of theoretical and experimental assumptions – it was at least solid enough for a large amount of funding and scientific time to be devoted to it. No doubt, once an agreed solution is reached, all the current uncertainties will vanish and scientists will again have the greatest confidence in these areas of science. What now has become 'unmade' will be 'remade'.

One way of thinking about what has happened is to treat Ray Davis' result itself as an experiment into the nature of science. It is as if Davis' result cuts a knife of uncertainty through the normal taken-for-granted ideas and practices. For a moment scientists could think the unthinkable, explore the unexplorable and cut loose from the shackles of normal science and just see 'what if . . .'. But if we take every suggestion seriously then nearly everything we take for granted is challenged. In this world the sun no longer has nuclear fusion as its source of energy; neutrinos oscillate, decay or stay within the sun; the sun experiences periods of mixing which correlate with ice ages; argon is trapped; weak interaction theory does not work; and so forth.

We have Ray Davis to thank for giving us this thought experiment in the plasticity of scientific culture. Of course, 'what-if science' is not conventional science; in ordinary science a million flowers most decidedly do not bloom. The puzzle the solar-neutrino problem leaves us with is the following: if scientists can in some circumstances think the unthinkable, what stops them doing it most of the time? If the answer does not lie in recalcitrant Nature, and throughout this book we have suggested that Nature imposes much less of a constraint than we normally imagine, this leaves scientific culture. Science works the way it does, not because of any absolute constraint from Nature, but because we make our science the way that we do.

Postscript 1992

The scientific jury on the solar-neutrino case is still out. Two second-generation experiments have reported results. SAGE is the Soviet–American Gallium Experiment using a detector containing 30 tonnes of pure gallium metal located under a mountain in the North Caucasus. GALLEX is an international collaboration using a huge tank of gallium chloride located under the Apennine Mountains in Italy. Both experiments should see between 124 and 132 SNU. SAGE has found only 20 SNU, whilst GALLEX has found 83 SNU. The

GALLEX result can be incorporated within standard solar models by 'severe stretching', but the SAGE result would need a more radical explanation such as neutrino oscillation. The conflicting results are explained by some scientists as being due to the difficulties of operating the pure gallium detector as opposed to the gallium chloride detector. Negotiations are in progress!

Conclusion: putting the golem to work

Looking forward and looking back

We have followed several episodes of science as they have unfolded. We have described not only the work of the most revered scientists, the Einsteins, Newtons and Pasteurs, but also work which it appears will not be acclaimed: Joseph Weber's high fluxes of gravity waves and Ungar and McConnell's memory transfer. In some of the cases examined – the solar-neutrino problem and the sexual behaviour of the whiptail lizard – the jury is still out. Will they make it into the scientific canon or will they be scientific cannon fodder? It remains to be seen, but don't expect to find the answer in the experiments and theories alone.

It is no accident that we have chosen to look at high science and low science together. We have tried to level out the scientific mountain range which rises up as a result of the forces of celebratory history. Look back whence we came in science and there are what seem to be unconquerable peaks – Mount Newton, Mount Pasteur, Mount Einstein – a mountain range of truth. But look forward and the terrain is flat. A few new foothills wrench themselves from the plain every time we glance backwards. What are those new peaks? Were they there yesterday? To understand how science works we must examine how we cause these foothills and mountains to emerge. To do this we must understand science which fails as well as science which succeeds. Only in this way will we have the courage to climb the forbidding mountains of yesterday, and those which are newly forming behind us. What our case studies show is that there is no logic of scientific discovery. Or, rather, if there is such a logic, it is the logic of everyday life.

Human error

It is impossible to separate science from society, yet preserving the idea that there are two distinct spheres is what creates the authoritarian image so familiar to most of us. How is it made to seem that the spheres are separate?

When something goes wrong with science, the scientific community reacts like a nest of ants with an intruder in their midst. Ants swarm over an intruder giving their lives for the nest; in the case of science it is human bodies that are sacrificed: the bodies of those responsible for the 'human error' that allowed the problem to arise. The space shuttle explodes because of human error; Chernobyl explodes because of human error. Finding the human error is the purpose of post-accident inquiries. By contrast, our conclusion is that human 'error' goes right to the heart of science, because the heart is made of human activity. When things go wrong, it is not because human error could have been avoided but because things will always go wrong in any human enterprise. One cannot ask of scientists and technologists that they be no longer human, yet only mythical automata – quite unlike the constituents of a golem – could deliver the sort of certainty that scientists have led us to expect of them.

As things stand, we have, as we remarked in the introduction, only two ways of thinking about science; it is all good or all bad. Unstable equilibrium – flip-flop thinking – is the inevitable consequence of a model of science and technology which is supposed to deliver complete certainty. The trouble is that both states of the flip-flop are to be feared. The overweening claims to authority of many scientists and technologists are offensive and unjustified but the likely reaction, born of failed promises, might precipitate a still worse anti-scientific movement. Scientists should promise less; they might then be better able to keep their promises. Let us admire them as craftspersons: the foremost experts in the ways of the natural world.

Public understanding of science

How does this view of science make a difference? The first point to stress, if it is not already clear, is that this is not an anti-science attitude. It should make very little difference to the way scientists act when they are doing their work at, metaphorically speaking, the laboratory bench. There is a sense in which the social view of science is useless to scientists – it can only weaken the driving force of the determination to discover. The impact of our redescriptions should be on the scientific method of those disciplines which ape what they take to be the way of going on in the high-prestige natural sciences, and on those individuals and organisations who would destroy fledgling sciences for their failure to live up to a misplaced ideal.

Notoriously, the social sciences suffer from the first malaise – physics envy, as it is known – with areas of experimental psychology and quantitative sociology, all pedantically stated hypotheses, and endless statistical manipulation of marginal data, being the most clear-cut examples of this kind of 'scientism'.

The second malaise is more worrisome. The favourable public reception of unusual sciences such as parapsychology – the study of 'mind over matter', 'telepathy', and the like – has given rise to fears that fringe sciences are taking over. An anti-fringe science movement has been spawned whose members take it on themselves to 'debunk' all that is not within the canon, in the name of proper scientific method. Where this effort is aimed at disabusing the public about unsupported claims, it is admirable, but the zeal of these self-appointed vigilantes carries over into areas where they have no business.

Recently, on British television, the public at large was able to witness a stage magician informing a prestigious scientist, head of a famous Paris institute, that his ideas were ridiculous. The motive for this attack was not the professor's methods but the topic he had chosen to research – homeopathy; the instrument of the attack was, nevertheless, an idealised version of what scientific method ought to be. It is no coincidence that those who feel most certain of their grip on scientific method have rarely worked on the frontiers of science themselves. There is a saying in love 'distance lends enchantment'; it is true of science too. It is important that these vigilante organisations do not become so powerful that they can stamp out all that is strange in the scientific world. Saving the public from charlatans is their role, but scientists must not use them to fight their battles for them. If homeopathy cannot be demonstrated experimentally, it is up to scientists, who know the risks of frontier research, to show why. To leave it to others is to court a different sort of golem – one who might destroy science itself.

Science and the citizen

The debate about the public understanding of science is equally confounded by confusion over method and content. What should be explained is methods of science, but what most people concerned with the issues want the public to know about is the truth about the natural world – that is, what the powerful believe to be the truth about the natural world. The laudable reason for concern with public understanding is that scientific and technological issues figure more and more in the political process. Citizens, when they vote, need to know enough to come to some decision about whether they prefer more coal mines or more nuclear power stations, more corn or clearer rivers, more tortured animals or more healthy children, or whether these really are the choices. Perhaps there are novel solutions: wave power, organic farming, drug testing without torture. The 'public understanders', as we might call them, seem to think that if the person in the street knows more science – as opposed to more *about* science – they will be able to make more sensible decisions about these things.

How strange that they should think this; it ranks among the great fallacies of our age. Why? – because PhDs and professors are found on all sides in these debates. The arguments have largely been invented in universities. Thus, all sides have expertise way beyond what can ever be hoped of the person in the street, and all sides know how to argue their case clearly and without obvious fallacies. Why such debates are unresolvable, in spite of all this expertise, is what we have tried to show in the descriptive chapters of this book. That is, we have shown that scientists at the research front cannot settle their disagreements through better experimentation, more knowledge, more advanced theories, or clearer thinking. It is ridiculous to expect the general public to do better.

We agree with the public understanders that the citizen needs to be informed enough to vote on technical issues, but the information needed is not about the content of science; it is about the relationship of experts to politicians, to the media, and to the rest of us. The citizen has great experience in the matter of how to cope with divided expertise – isn't this what party politics is? What the citizen cannot do is cope with divided expertise pretending to be something else. Instead of one question – 'Who to believe?' – there are two questions – 'Who to believe?' and 'Are scientists and technologists Gods or charlatans?'. The second question is what makes the whole debate so unstable because, as we have argued, there are only two positions available.

What we have tried to do here is dissolve the second question – scientists are neither Gods nor charlatans; they are merely experts, like every other expert on the political stage. They have, of course, their special area of expertise, the physical world, but their knowledge is no more immaculate than that of economists, health policy makers, police officers, legal advocates, weather forecasters, travel agents, car mechanics, or plumbers. The expertise that *we* need to deal with them is the well-developed expertise of everyday life; it is what we use when we deal with plumbers and the rest. Plumbers are not perfect – far from it – but society is not beset with anti-plumbers because being anti-plumbing is not a choice available to us. It is not a choice because the counter-choice, plumbing as immaculately conceived, is likewise not on widespread offer.

To change the public understanding of the political role of science and technology is the most important purpose of our book and that is why most of our chapters have revealed the inner workings of science.

Forensic science

It is not only where science and politics meet that there are implications for the understanding of science developed here. Wherever science touches on another institution things change when we learn to see science as expertise rather than as certain knowledge. Consider what happens when science and the law meet. In the courtroom scientific experts provide evidence touching upon a suspect's guilt or innocence. Was the hair found at the scene of the crime the same as the hair on the suspect's head? Were there fabric fibres in common? Could body fluids found on the victim have come from the accused, and how likely is it that they came from someone else? Had the accused handled explosives recently? At the time of writing, the British legal system is being rocked by a series of overturned legal verdicts in cases concerning bombs planted by the Irish Republican Army. Men and women have been locked up for many years, only for it to be discovered that the 'evidence' on which they were convicted was, to use the legal jargon 'unsafe'. Typically, the crucial evidence has been forensic science tests purporting to show that the accused had recently been handling nitroglycerine, indelible traces remaining on his or her hands. The trouble is, as it now turns out, the test is not infallible.

Other objects, such as playing cards, are made with chemicals related to nitroglycerine, and handling such objects might give rise to a positive test result. The forensic scientists involved in the trials did not report the possibility of these false positive readings, nor how likely they were to come about. The British forensic science profession, indeed the whole legal system, has lost credibility through these miscarriages of justice. Worse, it is probably the case that a number of innocent citizens suffered many years of unjust incarceration.

Comparing the analysis of method offered here with the conventional picture of science, it is easy to see how this disaster came about. As long as it is thought that science produces certainty, it seems inappropriate to treat scientific evidence like other legal evidence, so that disagreement *must*, once more, be blamed on human error. But it is the institutions in which forensic evidence is embedded that must take the blame. The problem is that it has not been seen to be necessary to have two versions of the evidence: a defence version and a prosecution version. Typically, in a British court, the Home Office alone supplies the scientists and the scientific conclusions. They present their seemingly neutral results to the court without prior detailed analysis by the defence. The scientific evidence should be neutral, so an alternative view is redundant – it is bound to come to the same conclusions! (To put it another way, scientists are not seen as *re*presenting, merely presenting.) But, as we have seen in the bombing scandals, contested forensic evidence is like contested scientific evidence everywhere; it is like the science described in this book. It is contestable.

The cost of having contested forensic evidence will be that science will no longer put a speedy end to legal trials. Instead of the law passing its responsibility over to the scientific experts, the scientific experts would be just one part of the contested legal process. But this is what *ought* to happen – it is unjust for it to be any other way. What is more, if scientific evidence is subject to the same contestation as other kinds of evidence, it cannot suffer the embarrassment of misplaced certainty.

Interestingly enough, in the American legal system things seem to have gone too far the other way. In the hands of a clever lawyer any piece of forensic evidence can be taken apart. Often forensic evidence carries no weight at all because lawyers have become so adept at finding so-called 'expert witnesses' who will 'deconstruct' each and every piece of scientific evidence. The new way of looking at science throws light upon what is happening here too.

In the first place we should not be surprised that any piece of evidence can be examined and doubted – this is what we should expect given the new understanding of science. It is not a matter of one side having an adequate grasp of the scientific facts and the other side being in error. Doubts about evidence can always be raised. But it does not follow from this that forensic evidence should carry no weight. In judging the merits of forensic evidence we have to apply the normal rules which we would apply if we were judging any argument between experts. For instance, some experts will have more credibility than others and some will have no credibility at all. What has happened in the American legal system seems to draw on only one lesson from the new view of science. Just because scientists disagree, and because experiments and observation alone cannot settle matters, does not mean that scientists do not reach agreement. Consider: gravity waves are not facts of the natural world, while the bending of star light by the sun is a fact.

What has to be thought about in the American legal system is how to bring about closure of debate now that scientists have lost so much credibility. Mechanisms will have to be found so that the influence of non-expert voices is not as great as that of experts. Of course, this will not be easy, especially when expertise is for hire to special interest groups. But solving such problems is the stuff of political and institutional life. American governmental agencies such as the Food and Drug Administration and the Environmental Protection Agency, and the American legal system as a whole, will only maintain credibility if they realise that science works by producing agreement among experts. Allowing everyone to speak is as bad as allowing a single group alone to speak. It is as bad as having no-one speak at all.

The trouble over forensic science can be seen as a microcosm of the whole debate. Claim too much for science and an unacceptable reaction is invited. Claim what can be delivered and scientific expertise will be valued or distrusted, utilised or ignored, not in an unstable way but just as with any other social institution.

Public inquiries

If we apply this new analysis everywhere that science touches on another social institution then a more useful understanding will emerge. What is happening when there are public enquiries about the building of a new nuclear power station? On the one hand there are experts producing complex calculations that seem to make the probability of an accident negligible. On the other hand, there are experts who consider the risk too awful to contemplate. One must take one's choice. Quasi-legal institutions, or Federal agencies, can help to sift and filter expert evidence but in the end the citizen can do no better than listen to both sides and decide in just the same way as one decides on where to buy a house; there is no way of being certain that one is not making a mistake.

Experiments or demonstrations in the public domain

When the Federal Aviation Authority crashed a plane filled with anti-misting kerosene to find out if it was a safer aviation fuel, and when

British Rail crashed a train into a nuclear fuel flask to find out whether it could be broken in an accident, they were not doing science. Experiments in real science hardly ever produce a clear-cut conclusion – that is what we have shown. What these agencies were doing were 'demonstrations' set up to settle a political debate. The role of science in such demonstrations is as dubious as it is in the one-sided British legal system.

At the very least, be suspicious if one interpretation of such a test is treated as though it were inevitable. Listen for interpretations from different interest groups, and make sure those groups are happy that they each had some control over how the test was set up, and what the result was taken to mean. If they do not agree on this, listen to the nature of their complaints.

Science on television

When science is described on television, watch out for the model of science that is implied. One television programme that came near to the sort of account we have given here revealed the trials and tribulations of the CERN team who discovered the fundamental 'Z' particle. The programme described the messiness of the apparatus, the false starts and the rebuildings, the uncertainties that attended the first results, the statistical calculations that were used to bolster certainty that something was being seen, the decision of the director to 'go public' in spite of the deep doubts of members of his team, and then the press conference in which a discovery announcement was made to the world. All this was wonderfully portrayed, but the last phrases of the narrator gave the game away. The programme was entitled, with a hint of self-conscious irony, let us hope, 'The Geneva *Event*', and the narrator looked back on what he had described as one of the greatest discoveries since the experiments of Faraday. Even here, then, the mess was not allowed to be the message. At the end triumphalism ruled. All too few television programmes offer the picture of science portrayed in these pages.

Accident inquiries

When public inquiries take place after accidents, as in the case of the space shuttle disaster, if they discover nothing but human error, beware. Discovering human error is attributing blame to something outside of science. It would be better if the blame were attributed to something inside – of course it will be humans who are to blame, but also not to blame. No-one is perfect. If the officials who allowed the frozen shuttle to fly that fateful morning had listened to every warning they were offered at every launch, then the space plane would never have flown. Science and technology are inherently risky. When responsibility for trouble is attributed to particular individuals it should be done in the same spirit as political responsibility is attributed; in politics, responsibility is not quite the same as fault. We may be sure that there are many accidents waiting to happen and many more heads will roll, but there is simply nothing we can do about it.

Science education

Finally we come to science education in schools. It is nice to know the content of science – it helps one to do a lot of things such as repair the car, wire a plug, build a model aeroplane, use a personal computer to some effect, know where in the oven to put a soufflé, lower one's energy bills, disinfect a wound, repair the kettle, avoid blowing oneself up with the gas cooker, and much much more. For that tiny proportion of those we educate who will go on to be professional research scientists, knowledge of the content of science must continue to be just as rigorous and extended, and perhaps blinkered, as it is now. But for most of our children, the future citizens of a technological society, there is another, and easier, lesson to be learned.

Every classroom in which children are conducting the same experiment in unison is a microcosm of frontier science. Each such multiple encounter with the natural world is a self-contained sociological experiment in its own right. Think about what happens: the teacher asks the class to discover the boiling point of water by inserting a thermometer into a beaker and taking a reading when the water is steadily boiling. One thing is certain: almost no-one will get 100 °C unless they already know the answer, and they are trying to please the teacher. Skip will get 102 °C, Tania will get 105 °C, Johnny will get 99.5 °C, Mary will get 100.2 °C, Zonker will get 54 °C, while Brian will not quite manage to get a result; Smudger will boil the beaker dry and burst the thermometer. Ten minutes before the end of the experiment the teacher will gather these scientific results and start the social engineering. Skip had his thermometer in a bubble of superheated steam when he took his reading, Tania had some impurities in her water, Johnny did not allow the beaker to come fully to the boil, Mary's result showed the effect of slightly increased atmospheric pressure above sea-level, Zonker, Brian and Smudger have not yet achieved the status of fully competent research scientists. At the end of the lesson, each child will be under the impression that their experiment has proved that water boils at exactly 100 °C, or would have done were it not for a few local difficulties that do not affect the grown-up world of science and technology, with its fully trained personnel and perfected apparatus.

That ten minutes renegotiation of what really happened is the important thing. If only, now and again, teachers and their classes would pause to reflect on that ten minutes they could learn most of what there is to know about the sociology of science. For that ten minutes illustrates better the tricks of professional frontier science than any university or commercial laboratory with its well-ordered predictable results. Eddington, Michelson, Morley, Weber, Davis, Fleischmann, Pons, Jones, McConnell, Ungar, Crews, Pasteur and Pouchet are Skips, Tanias, Johnnys, Marys, Zonkers, Brians, and Smudgers with clean white coats and 'PhD' after their names. They all come up with wildly varying results. There are theorists hovering around, like the schoolteacher, to explain and try to reconcile. In the end, however, it is the scientific community (the head teacher?) who brings order to this chaos, transmuting the clumsy antics of the collective Golem Science into a neat and tidy scientific myth. There is nothing wrong with this; the only sin is not knowing that it is always thus.

References and further reading

Atkinson, P. and Delamont, S. (1977) 'Mock-ups and Cock-ups: The Stage Management of Guided Discovery Instruction', in P. Woods, and M. Hammersley (eds.) *School Experience: Explorations in the Sociology of Education*, London: Croom Helm

Bennett, E. L. and Calvin, M. (1964) 'Failure to Train Planarians Reliably', *Neurosciences Research Program Bulletin*, July–August, 3–24

Bijker, W., Hughes, T. P. and Pinch, T. J. (1987) (eds.) *The Social Construction of Technological Systems*, Cambridge, Mass.: MIT Press

Bloor, D. (1991) *Knowledge and Social Imagery*, 2nd edition, Chicago and London: University of Chicago Press

Byrne, W. L., Samuel, D., Bennett, E. L., Rosenzwieg, M. R., Wasserman, E., Wagner, A. R., Gardner, F., Galambos, R., Berger, B. D., Margoulis, D. L., Fenischel, R. L., Stein, L., Corson, J. A., Enesco, H. E., Chorover, S. L., Holt, C. E. III, Schiller, P. H., Chiapetta, L., Jarvik, M. E., Leaf, R. C., Dutcher, J. D., Horovitz, Z. P. and Carlton, P. L. (1966) 'Memory Transfer', *Science*, 153, 658–9

Close, F. (1991) *Too Hot to Handle: The Race for Cold Fusion*, Princeton University Press

Collins, H. M. (1981) (ed.) *Knowledge and Controversy*, special issue of *Social Studies of Science*, 11, No. 1

Collins, H. M. (1985), *Changing Order: Replication and Induction in Scientific Practice*, London and Beverley Hills: Sage; second edition with a new afterword published by Chicago University Press, 1992

Collins, H. M. (1990) *Artificial Experts: Social Knowledge and Intelligent Machines*, Cambridge, Mass.: MIT Press

Collins, H. M. and Pinch, T. J. (1982) *Frames of Meaning: the Social Construction of Extraordinary Science*, London: Routledge.

Collins, H. M. and Shapin, S. (1989) 'Experiment, Science Teaching and the New History and Sociology of Science', in M. Shortland and A. Warwick (eds.) *Teaching the History of Science*, London: Blackwell

Corning, W. C. and Riccio, D. (1970) 'The Planarian Controversy', in W. L. Byrne (ed.) *Molecular Approaches to Learning and Memory*, New York: Academic Press, pp. 107–49

Dubos, R. (1960) *Louis Pasteur: Free Lance of Science*, English edition: New York: Charles Scribner's

Earman, J. and Glymour, C. (1980) 'Relativity and Eclipses: The British Eclipse Expeditions of 1919 and their Predecessors', *Historical Studies in the Physical Sciences*, 11 (1), 49–85

Einstein, A. and Infeld, L. (1938) *The Evolution of Physics: From Early Concepts to Relativity and Quanta*, New York: Simon and Schuster

Farley, J. and Geison, G. L. (1974) 'Science Politics and Spontaneous Generation in Nineteenth-Century France: the Pasteur–Pouchet Debate', *Bulletin for the History of Medicine*, 48, 161–98. (Referenced page numbers are from the version of this paper reprinted in Collins, H. M. (1982) (ed.) *The Sociology of Scientific Knowledge: A Sourcebook*, Bath University Press)

Fleck, L. (1979) *Genesis and Development of a Scientific Fact*, Chicago and London: University of Chicago Press

Gieryn, T. (1992) 'The Ballad of Pons and Fleischmann: Experiment and Narrative in the (Un)Making of Cold Fusion', in Ernan McMullin (ed.) *The Social Dimensions of Science*, Notre Dame University Press

Goldstein, A. (1973) 'Comments on the "Isolation, Identification and Synthesis of a Specific-Behaviour-Inducing Brain Peptide" ', *Nature*, **242**, 60–2

Goldstein, A., Sheehan, P. and Goldstein, P. (1971) 'Unsuccessful Attempts to Transfer Morphine Tolerance and Passive Avoidance by Brain Extracts', *Nature*, 233, 126–9

Gooding, D., Pinch, T. and Schaffer, S. (1989) *The Uses of Experiment*, Cambridge University Press

Haraway, D. (1989) *Primate Visions: Gender, Race, and Nature in the World of Modern Science*, London and New York, Routledge

Hawking, S. (1988) *A Brief History of Time: From the Big Bang to Black Holes*, Bantam Books

Jasanoff, S. (1991) *The Fifth Branch*, Cambridge, MA: Harvard University Press

Kuhn, T. S. (1972) *The Structure of Scientific Revolutions*, Chicago: University of Chicago Press

Latour, B. (1984) *Science in Action*, Milton Keynes and Cambridge, Mass.: Open University Press and Harvard University Press

Latour, B. and Woolgar, S. (1979) *Laboratory Life*, London and Beverley Hills: Sage

Lewenstein, B. (1992) 'Cold Fusion and Hot History', *Osiris*, 7 (in press)

Mallove, E. (1991) *Fire From Ice: Searching for the Truth Behind The Cold Fusion Furore*, New York: John Wiley

McConnell, J. V. (1962) 'Memory Transfer Through Cannibalism in Planarians', *Journal of Neurophysiology*, 3, 42–8

McConnell, J. V. (1965) 'Failure to Interpret Planarian Data Correctly: A Reply to Bennett and Calvin', unpublished manuscript, Ann Arbor: University of Michigan

Miller, D. C. (1933) 'The Ether Drift Experiment and the Determination of the Absolute Motion of the Earth', *Reviews of Modern Physics*, 5, 203–42

Myers, G. (1990) *Writing Biology: Texts in the Social Construction of Scientific Knowledge*, Madison: University of Wisconsin Press

Pickering, A. (1984) *Constructing Quarks*, Chicago: University of Chicago Press

Pinch, T. J. (1986) *Confronting Nature: The Sociology of Solar-Neutrino Detection*, Dordrecht: Reidel

Richards, E. (1991) *Vitamin C and Cancer: Medicine or Politics*, London: Macmillan

Shapin, S. and Schaffer, S. (1985) *Leviathan and the Air-Pump: Hobbes, Boyle and the Experimental Life*, Princeton University Press

Swenson, L. S. (1972) *The Ethereal Aether: A History of the Michelson-Morley-Miller Aether-Drift Experiments, 1880–1930*, Austin and London: University of Texas Press

Travis, G. D. L. 'Memories and Molecules: A Sociological History of the Memory Transfer Phenomenon', PhD Thesis, University of Bath, 1987

Ungar, G. (1973) 'The Problem of Molecular Coding of Neural Information: A Critical Review', *Naturwissenschaften*, 60, 307–12

Ungar, G, Desiderio, D. M., and Parr, W. (1972) 'Isolation, Identification and synthesis of a specific-behaviour-inducing Brain Peptide. *Nature*, 238, 198–202

Von Kluber, H. (1960) 'The Determination of Einstein's Light-deflection in the Gravitational Field of the Sun', *Vistas of Astronomy*, 3, 47–77

Index